COMMUNICATION STRATEGIES FOR ADMINISTRATIVE PROFESSIONALS

How to Communicate What You Can Do, Can't Do, Will Do, Won't Do, Need and Want

By

Karen Porter

Coach and Advisor to Administrative Professionals
and Founder and President of The Effective Admin
and Virtual Association for Administrative Professionals

http://www.TheEffectiveAdmin.com
http://www.TheVAAP.com

Albee Publishing Company, LLC

For my husband, Rob, who provides encouragement and reminds me to focus.

Table of Contents

Preface

When writing this book, my focus was on delivering practical information you can use on the job or in your career and not simply theory. I've been serving practical information to administrative professionals through *The Effective Admin* brand of resources since 2004. Even before then I provided practical information in articles published in trade periodicals geared toward the workplace, including some specifically for administrative professionals. I've never been a fan of solely theoretical information.

Perhaps like you, when I seek guidance I want people to give me examples of scenarios and information that applies to me with tips for implementing that information. For instance, describe a situation and tell me what I might say and what I shouldn't say (or do or not do) to get the results I want or need. And make it realistic. When I read a suggested conversation for the workplace, I don't want to be thinking, "Seriously, who would really say that!"

The advice I read and write needs to pass my reality "smell test." I was an employee in the workplace for over 18 years prior to owning my current business advising administrative professionals for 10 years; therefore, I personally know that more than theory is needed to navigate in the workplace environment. This book gives you that "hands-on" advice to use in your workplace and your administrative role and career. Use it as is or modify it and use it as you see fit.

I wish you much success in your administrative role and career.

Sincerely,
Karen Porter

Introduction

This book is about communication strategies for *administrative professionals*. The latter phrase encompasses all types of assistants and administrative assistance in particular. So if you are an administrative assistant, executive assistant, or similar title or role, then this book is for you. In particular, you'll read about some situations faced daily, or periodically, by administrative professionals in general in the workplace and in their administrative careers that call for strategic communication.

You'll be given some strategic communication scripts and examples of how to communicate in particular situations that you can put in your "tool box." You can tweak these communication strategies and use them in the workplace and in your administrative career.

The phrase *communication strategy* in this book means you think – strategize – before you communicate. You plan what you will say or write. It doesn't mean anything with a manipulative tone. It means strategize in an authentic manner to get the results you're looking for with your communication. Those results could be presenting yourself and your role in a clear, positive and meaningful way when people ask you about what you do for a living, or within your company. Also, you may communicate strategically to try to become more visible or to convey your accomplishments to those that matter (usually your managers). This takes communication strategies. You don't want to "wing it" when talking about what you do or have done. Usually, that won't flatter you or serve your goals. Unprepared people wing it. Spontaneity isn't a communication strategy in business.

You'll also want to use communication strategies to communicate what you can do, such as if you want broader responsibilities or your executive to delegate more to you. You'll need communication strategies to communicate what you can't do, such as work on two managers' jobs simultaneously (there is multitasking and there is impossible; that is the latter). Also, in order to stay satisfied in your administrative role and career, you have to like it and enjoy going to work. You can't do that if you're being worked to death, figuratively speaking. However, rather than whine about an overwhelming workload, you can use communication strategies to present your situation to your manager in a positive manner that gets you the results you want: a workable solution to your dilemma. This will keep you off the road to job and career burnout and on the road to job and career satisfaction. Plus you'll get your work done!

If you have a new manager or executive – new to you or to his or her role – you'll learn communication strategies for letting that person know what you will do for him or her in your administrative role and as that person's direct assistant. So many managers or executives don't know, but also don't want to ask. Just like you, managers and executives want to present themselves in the best light. Some are uncomfortable admitting they don't know how to utilize an assistant. "Guessing" by either party is never a good communication strategy. That's similar to "winging it" on the job.

Other times as an assistant you'll need to communicate strategically what you won't do, such as during ethical dilemmas. You don't want to dismiss someone else's values and morals, but you don't want to dismiss your own either; you have to live with memories of your actions permanently, while jobs are temporary and careers are secondary to your true self and substance. Jobs are something you do; they are not your make-up. Ethical dilemmas, as well as other types of personal and professional boundaries, call for communication strategies in the workplace best not left to the last moment. Communicating boundaries helps you to establish business partnerships with your managers and executives.

There also will be situations where you will need to communicate "no." Many of us need to learn how to say no. While no is a simple word and many people pride themselves on saying it to your face, as an administrative professional you likely already know that you need to use tact and diplomacy. Clarity and directness go hand in hand, but in-your-face directness is not always a smart communication strategy, despite the bragging from those people who will tell you they just say "no" and walk away.

Administrative professionals always use clarity, direct communication, and tact and diplomacy, whether communicating with managers, executives, coworkers, company customers or vendors. A good communication strategy is indispensable in these situations. That means think before you speak to get the results you're seeking, to communicate the right message, and to leave the other party feeling respected and amicable. The latter is important in your role especially as an administrative professional because it's important that you have a wide network to do your job effectively. Build those relationships with communication strategies; don't tear them down with thoughtless words and phrases.

Furthermore, as an assistant you undoubtedly will have to communicate what you can't say and won't say. You are privy to lots of confidential information. Some is so subtle and integrated into your daily work day with your manager or executive and for your company that you may not even realize the information is best kept to yourself – or that you are releasing it. As an assistant, and especially applicable to the higher level of assistant, you must recognize when you're about to give out more information than you're taking in and learn to maintain confidences. Utilizing genuine communication strategies – and being able to recognize a few underhanded ones – will help you maintain confidences and communicate what you can't or won't say. Sometimes you can't say because you don't know. Regardless of the specifics of why you can't say what you can't say, you'll find useful examples of phrasing to cover these situations further along in this book (chapter 8, specifically).

Further onward (chapters 9-10), you'll find some communication strategies for communicating what you need on the job and what you want in your career. These are two different things comprising many different scenarios, but both your needs and your wants affect your job and career satisfaction – and thus your life. While some administrative professionals have told me they don't believe being satisfied or dissatisfied on the job affects one's home life, I know better (firsthand and from listening to stories from other administrative professionals).

A happy, satisfied day at work sets the tone for your personal satisfaction at home. When you're not satisfied at work or unhappy in your career, you "take it home" and you tell others (who usually don't want to hear about it). In turn, your mood wreaks havoc on your personal life and daily satisfaction. This is because you are *not* two different people: the work you and the personal, home life you. You are one person, and though we all like to think we leave our problems at the door at work and enter with a smile and vice versa, that's not happening if you're human. So it is important to get what you need and want on the job and in your career in order to be satisfied overall in your life.

Again, that is because you have just one life; not a work life and a home life. Therefore, learn and use these communication strategies in this section of the book to ask for what you need and want in your role and career. For sure, you won't get what you don't ask for. While this is just a small sampling in this book of situations in which you should communicate your needs and wants, it's a start. Communication strategies start with small steps. Learn some, implement them, and soon you'll be able to write your own book on what works and doesn't work in regard to communication strategies for administrative professionals.

That small sampling of situations discussing communicating your specific wants and needs is not the end of this book. Everything mentioned above so far is what I promised in the subtitle of this book which was *How to Communicate What You Can Do, Can't Do, Will Do, Won't Do, Need and Want.* I've also added a chapter on how to communicate with questions; the right ones can get you the results you are seeking from your communication, and the wrong ones will lead you to a dead end. Plus there are two chapters about communicating with e-mail and other electronic forms of communication. Lastly, you'll learn about the importance of communicating with professionalism and what that means in regard to your communication strategies as an administrative professional.

Each chapter also has a "Chapter Recap" section at its end. Please don't think you can read this bullet-point list and skip the details in each chapter. These chapter recaps only cover some major points made in the chapters. They do not include the examples or some of the important elaboration on the topic that's in each chapter's body of text. The chapter recaps simply reinforce several points you learned in the chapter. Think of the chapter recaps as learning aids.

After the chapters, there are appendices with assorted information relevant to the text of this book but more supplemental in nature. The information is geared toward helping you with your communication strategies. The first appendix has excerpts from my newsletter, *The Effective Admin*, of some short communication strategies. This includes potential responses you can use in certain scenarios such as to halt gossip in your presence or unsavory humor and to respond to compliments or disagree politely. Use any or all of these communication tactics and phrases. Test them out. Keep what works for you and not the rest.

If you encounter some scenarios as an administrative professional not listed, send them along to me for my future reference when I update this book (karen@albeepublishing.com). I probably already have a communication strategy for that situation (or will find one). If you're facing a situation in need of a good communication strategy, your administrative colleagues likely are too. Therefore, I may want to mention the scenario and potential communication solutions in future editions. Meanwhile, if you're looking for more information to help you in your administrative profession after reading this book, then see appendix I; it describes another resource produced by me for administrative professionals.

Without further ado, let's get to the actual communication strategies promised to you in this book...

Chapter 1

The Skill You Need
to Communicate Strategically

It would be remiss to start offering communication strategies without telling you about the one skill you will need in order to utilize most of the strategies. That skill is assertiveness. More specifically, it's positive assertion skills.

Many administrative professionals do not have this skill (and the same for many non-admins). Fortunately, assertiveness can be learned if it does not come naturally to you as one of your personal attributes. It is important that you do learn how to be assertive. Every administrative assistant or executive assistant needs to behave assertively at various times in the workplace. There is no getting around that fact if you want to be really good at your job and in your administrative role. The use or lack of positive assertion also can affect your happiness and satisfaction with your job and administrative career.

Why Admins Need to Be Assertive

In the workplace, positive assertion is a tool – part of your communication strategy tool kit.

- Assertiveness is a tool that allows you to ask for what you need to do your job or to achieve the quality results you want or need for a task or project.
- Assertiveness is the skill that helps you develop a more harmonious and more productive relationship with your manager or executive, coworkers, and external customers.
- Assertiveness is what allows you to renegotiate deadlines when you have an overflowing workload.

- Assertiveness is the skill you need to ask vendors for a lower rate or complimentary perk in your dealings with them.
- Assertiveness is the skill you need to initiate a productive conversation with your manager or a potential employer about your salary.
- Assertiveness is the tool you use to tell someone tactfully that you can't help her today or perhaps ever.
- Assertiveness is also the tool you use to speak up and tell someone that you can and would like to help her.

There are literally hundreds of situations for which you should be using assertive behavior in the workplace and as an administrative professional. You don't have to be born assertive (no one is); you can learn to be assertive with knowledge and practice, practice, and more practice.

Let's Define Assertiveness Further

Assertiveness is a behavior style in which you freely express your feelings, opinions and needs, and you do so in a way that respects the feelings, opinions and needs of the person with whom you're interacting. You can make these expressions without feeling guilty, anxious or embarrassed. You have that right. That's part of what being assertive is about.

Positive assertion also includes your right and ability to say "no" and to feel good about your decision – all without trampling on the other person's rights and while leaving that person feeling good about the interaction too.

Assertiveness should not be confused with aggressiveness or passive aggressiveness. Those are not desirable professional behaviors. Some administrative professionals mistakenly say that they believe they need to learn to behave more aggressively at work to get their needs and wants met and to be visible and heard; they really mean to say "behave more assertively."

While you may feel like you're going into battle on an occasion at work, you're not and do not need to behave aggressively toward anyone in the workplace. However, to communicate strategically with your managers, coworkers, customers and vendors, you will at times need to behave assertively.

Assertiveness also should not be confused with passiveness. If you let things happen to you and around you when you should be responding or giving input, you are certainly not behaving assertively. You are behaving passively. You will not get your workplace needs met. No one will even know they exist. Problems and issues may arise in your work and output.

An example of positive assertion vs. aggressiveness, passive aggressiveness or passiveness is in this workplace scenario:

Your executive asks you to stay late to help her work on a report she is behind in completing that is due tomorrow afternoon. However, you know that you need to leave on time because you have a personal appointment after work that's important to you.

If you respond to your executive in this situation with *positive assertion*, you will explain to her that you cannot stay late due to an important personal commitment that can't be rescheduled. You will explain this using a normal, neutral tone and perhaps expressing genuine disappointment that you can't help her in this situation. You will be polite and respectful. However, you also will remain firm in what you can't do (and know it is your right to say no in order to meet your needs). You may offer an alternative idea in order to make the outcome of this conversation work for both of your needs. For instance, you may offer to complete part of the report for her later at home during the evening or suggest that you come in two hours early tomorrow to work on it.

If you respond *aggressively* in this situation, you may say something that stems from frustration. This is especially if this last-minute scenario has become all too common with your executive, and you tend to lash out when you're tired at the end of a work day. So you may say: "You're down to the wire again! I'm sorry; I just can't help you this time. I have an appointment in 30 minutes. You're on your own this time. Sorry!" Or perhaps you just look at your executive, pause, stare for a few seconds and roll your eyes (gestures can be aggressive too) and then say, "You really need help tonight! Really!"

Or you may take a *passive aggressive* route. That's one in which you say, "Sure, I'll stay and help," and then you rush through the report, putting it together sloppily or assuring your executive what she wrote sounds top-notch when you know it truly stinks. You're just doing what it takes to get out of there quicker, right? And this time your executive will learn a lesson about waiting until the last minute to prepare a report when the committee reads it tomorrow and tells her it flat out stinks. You think: "Oops! You should've started working on it earlier! Hee, hee."

And finally, *passive* behavior would be if you just plop back down in your desk chair, staying late to do your executive's work with her while knowing you are missing your very important personal commitment. You just can't say no or offer options. Your thoughts are that you don't like to make waves or cause conflict. And she is "the boss," you think. Who says no to their boss, right? So you try to hide your unhappiness and stress at knowing you're about to miss your own appointment and put your hand out for the work. "Let's do it," you say to your executive.

Of all those options, only one is the right one for you to choose in this scenario and that is the first one presented which is positive assertion. To reach your full potential in your administrative role and career, you must practice positive assertion. To be a genuine, long-term asset to your manager, executive or company, you must practice positive assertion. It's the most important tool you need in your communication strategies toolkit. You can learn to use this tool, or use it better than you do now if you already have some natural ability with behaving assertively.

See Appendix B for a chart with the differences and similarities of assertive, passive, aggressive, and passive aggressive behavior.

When you become assertive, or more assertive than you are now, you will find your business relationships may change. Your interactions may take a different tone and it will be a professional tone. You may even find people notice you more. And they will certainly respect you more when you practice positive assertion. That's a guarantee! You will be more effective in your administrative role. Try it and see.

Behaving assertively in the work place helps you to take charge of your work life. Things don't just "happen" to you, and you don't just "react" to things anymore. You make things happen, and you respond with deliberation to people and situations. Many of the communication strategies in the following chapters involve behaving assertively and some include assertive dialogue examples. Use them guilt-free!

***

Chapter 1 Recap:

- Positive assertion skills are necessary to carry out many communication strategies in the workplace and in your career.
- Every administrative professional needs to behave assertively at times in the workplace.
- Assertiveness is a tool that allows you to ask for what you need or want on the job and in your career.
- Assertive behavior can be learned. Nobody is born assertive (though some people may have some natural ability with this skill or attribute).
- More specifically, assertiveness is a behavior style in which you freely express your feelings, opinions and needs, and you do so in a way that respects the feelings, opinions and needs of the person with whom you're interacting.
- Positive assertion includes your right and ability to say "no."
- Assertiveness should not be confused with aggressiveness or passive aggressiveness; neither are good behaviors. Nor should assertiveness be confused with passiveness, which is meek behavior.
- To reach your full potential in your administrative role and career you must practice positive assertion.

- When you become assertive, or more assertive than you are now, your business interactions may take on a more professional tone.
- Behaving assertively in the workplace helps you to take charge of your work life.

Chapter 2

Communicating What You Do

As the administrative professional in your office, department or company, you may well be "the glue that holds your office together," and you likely "wear many hats." But you are much more than a cliché. Therefore, you should describe your role to others in terms other than clichés.

"A trite phrase or expression" (per *The Merriam-Webster Dictionary*) does not explain your administrative role with the impact it deserves. You are a unique professional. How you explain to others what your role is, what you do in your role, and why it's of value reflects on your professionalism and ability to communicate. Try the following communication strategies when defining to others who you are in the company.

So What Do You Do?

Picture this: You're seated at a workplace dinner, or even standing in the elevator or hallway, and the person next to you asks, "So what do you do?" Or perhaps one day your manager or executive asks you to give him a list of what you do.

Your first inclination may be to start rattling off specific activities like you answer customer phone inquiries, make airline and hotel reservations for staff members, and book speakers and catering for company events.

However, while you do those "tasks," you may want to respond in broader terms of "responsibilities." That is, you communicate with customers, coordinate trips for staff, and manage company event details. You do *tasks* to fulfill your *responsibilities.*

You're Much More Than "Just the Admin"

"Oh, I see, you're just the admin," says someone you're mingling with at a workplace event. Or perhaps it's a coworker deep in conversation with you about the ups and downs of the workplace who carelessly says: "...but you don't have to worry about these things because you're just the admin."

Thoughtless? Sure. Malicious intention? Probably not. Uneducated about what "the admin" does? For sure. Don't take it personally. It's about that person and his or her thought processes and not you. After all, you know who you are, what you do, what's important about your job and why your administrative role is valuable to companies.

So how should you respond? Firstly, know you don't have to *react* to every comment made to you. Make it your choice to respond. Then if you decide to respond, calmly and pleasantly ask for clarification: "I don't get what you mean by, 'You're just the admin.' Can you explain that further?"

Put the other person at ease by using a non-confrontational tone and manner. When you keep the conversation going, you have an opportunity to understand that person's perception of "just the admin," while also educating that person on the perks of being an administrative professional and the value of having one in the department or company.

The Elevator Pitch Formula for Admins

An "elevator pitch" is a slang phrase for that 30-second statement you make about a person, product or service during small talk with someone in an elevator, at a party, at a job fair, while escorting someone to see your executive, or while walking down the hallway together.

In your case as an administrative professional, your elevator pitch is your response to "So what do you do." It's your response to "What's your role at the company?" and similar questions delivered during pleasantries or occasions calling for small talk. A few fools may use the question in a nosy kind of way or to weed out people they don't want to mingle with at workplace events who they (perhaps incorrectly) believe can't "forward their careers." However, most people truly are just being friendly and inquisitive for authentic reasons.

Many people often have trouble conceiving opening statements to make small talk at work-related events. Questions about your role are simply easy conversation starters that come to mind for those people. Unfortunately, such questions about what you do can be easy for others to ask but hard for you to answer impromptu, especially if your job is administrative professional and you do a lot of everything. If you've never thought through the question and response, then you may answer awkwardly or defer the question lamely: "Oh, I'm the administrative professional in our office, and I do a little of everything; whatever is needed. How about you? What do you do?"

To answer with more confidence and clarity, plan some responses now. Here's a fill-in-the-blank formula to help you:

I work with <u>John Doe</u> to <u>keep him organized</u>. This is how <u>together we see results like the xyz last week</u>.

I work with [who or what department] to [do what]. This is how [we do what or get what results].

That's just one elevator pitch possibility but one that will work for you when making small talk at networking or work-related events and luncheons. Fill in the blanks and tweak what goes in the blanks to your satisfaction. Practice saying your elevator pitch a few times in the mirror too so you're ready when the "impromptu" moment comes.

Also, update your elevator pitch periodically. Even create a few different pitches that are phrased for different audiences. For instance, you might say something different to a new coworker while casually strolling into the office together from the parking lot than you would say at a job fair or to someone you thought of as a potential employer.

Each pitch is still an authentic response to "So what do you do," but you're focusing the response toward the audience. After all, as already stated you do a lot of things. Therefore, you can say your elevator pitch in many different ways and it'll still be authentic. Write several pitches in your private notes so you won't forget them. You can review them now and then, especially before a networking event.

***

Chapter 2 Recap:

- Administrative professionals are more than clichés (e.g. "glue that holds your office together"). Therefore, describe your role in terms other than clichés.
- How you explain to others what your role is and its value reflects on your professionalism and ability to communicate.
- Rather than rattling off specific activities or tasks to explain what you do when asked, respond in broader terms of "responsibilities."
- You don't have to react or respond to people who say, "...but you're just the admin." However, you can choose to do so. Continue the conversation by asking for clarification, using neutral language and tone.
- Conversations started by "just the admin" comments give you opportunities to correct misinformed perceptions of the administrative role and educate the misinformed speakers about what you *really* do.
- Create and rehearse a 30-second statement – an "elevator pitch" – to use at networking functions so you can respond with confidence and clarity to small talk such as, "So what do you do?"
- Update your elevator pitch periodically and write a few different statements to potentially use with different types of audiences (e.g. luncheon of coworkers vs. job fair).
- Your elevator pitch should always be authentic.

Chapter 3

Communicating What You've Done

It's important to know and be able to communicate your accomplishments in your administrative role and career. While you feel good when you accomplish something, you should also know that your accomplishments are often results too, and results are important to employers. Results help employers determine who is worthy of a promotion, raise or open position. Accomplishments and results can lead to new opportunities for interesting assignments. Plus accomplishments and results show your current employer that you are doing useful and valuable things in the company; you are not just an "overhead expense" adding indirect or no value to the company who shows up and fills a seat. Indeed you are not!

However, many administrative professionals do not understand their true value in their administrative roles or to a company. Similarly, they don't see their accomplishments. In other words, the value, accomplishments and results may be there but they don't see them. And finally, if they do understand their accomplishments and see them, they don't want to talk about them out loud. This is true of administrative professionals but also of many women in general, of which there are many in the administrative field. Some of these administrative professionals view talking about their own accomplishments as bragging, and they do not view bragging favorably. They'd much rather wait for someone else to "brag" about them.

While it's true that recommendations and endorsements from third parties (e.g. your manager, coworkers, colleagues, and company's customers) carry reputable weight on your behalf, it's also true that you could be waiting a long time for those people to speak up for and about you. Do not be too demure in your workplace or you will be invisible. Start the cycle of talk on your behalf. Brag a little about your expertise and value to the company, but in a subtle and professional way. Self-promote!

Take a bow for your accomplishments when they happen because if you don't grab your own credit, sometimes someone else will. Don't fume when that person talks about the project you both worked on while leaving out one detail: you! Instead, learn communication strategies for discussing what you've done: your accomplishments and results.

Let's Talk Accomplishments

Before you can strategically communicate what you've done (i.e. your accomplishments), you have to be able to see and define those accomplishments. However, you may be thinking: "So what have I done that can be communicated as an accomplishment? I create spreadsheets, answer phones, and do a variety of miscellaneous tasks for my manager. I don't accomplish things per se; I do daily tasks."

You may be thinking that, and if so your thinking is wrong. You work on projects probably too. Plus many of those daily tasks can be <u>bundled</u> into *accomplishments* and *results* too. The latter is *goals*. Did you know that? That's right; accomplishments and results can be goals. You achieve accomplishments and results; goals are achievements. That's helpful to know because many administrative professionals are being asked by their managers and executives to list workplace goals, especially during performance appraisal sessions.

So when you're answering the phone year-round, you're not just talking on the telephone daily. By year-end you may have answered 90% of all incoming calls live by the third ring and/or resolved 50 customers' issues by the end of a work day or 500 by the end of the year. That's an accomplishment.

So is successfully organizing five all-hands meetings in a year. Or maybe you coordinated an annual charity gala that raised $100,000, while decreasing the expenses as defined the previous year.

Or perhaps you increased the visibility and goodwill in your community for your company when you spoke on behalf of the company to three community organizations during the year, or when you organized and completed a company volunteer food drive.

Then there are all those matters you handled related to money. You achieved some great savings overall in coordinating travel for those you support. In fact, according to your notes (kept year-round by item), you coordinated 45 trips for all the staff you support over a twelve-month period and negotiated hotel rate discounts or other savings of $7,500 while doing it. You brought the travel budget down by your intended 2% goal this year vs. last year's baseline figure for travel expenses. Yea!

And you not only prepared PowerPoint slide presentations during the year, but you prepared 30 of them; half were used to gain the company new clients according to the associates who used them. You know this because you followed up on the outcome of these presentations with your colleagues. Sure, you didn't go out and give the presentation or line up the gig (or maybe you did the latter), but you contributed to this company success. Your achievement was part of the bigger picture. Put yourself in that bigger picture whenever possible. Connect the dots for your managers and executives. Put yourself in the big picture. Put yourself on the team.

Keep a personal folder that you add your accomplishments to ongoing. Don't try to remember all of your accomplishments. They won't be top of mind when you need to showcase them or discuss them. Memories aren't reliable. Keep a running list or journal of your accomplishments. Put any supporting paperwork in the folder or binder too. Never stop doing this. Do it throughout your career. Take this folder with you from job to job, figuratively speaking. In reality, keep this folder or binder at home and not in your office. Or keep a master copy in both places. This information is way too valuable to lose, whether a digital or paper file.

How to Verbally Toot Your Own Horn Subtly

There are communication strategies for doing self-promotion without seemingly doing the kind of bragging that has a negative connotation to it. Verbal self-promotion by you can occur at the copy machine while talking to someone helping you, as an attendee in a staff meeting, chatting with your supervisor while volunteering at an invent, during conversation in a performance review session with your manager, or walking down the hallway with your manager's manager.

So the *when* and *where* is less important than the *how* to do it and *how long* to do it. Just *intentionally* do it now and then. Below are some communication strategies covering the "how" and "how long."

Keep your self-promotion comments short.

Mention something you've done in a relevant conversation, but don't ramble or take over the conversation, making it a monologue. Say it briefly. Pause. Let the other person speak. If that person is intrigued, she can say "Tell me more." Otherwise, she heard. Keep the conversation what it should be: two-way communication. There will be other conversations.

Example

MANAGER: How was your friend's wedding?

YOU: Exciting. The photographer she hired got food poisoning the night before so I volunteered to do his job.

MANAGER: Wow. What a responsibility.

YOU: For some, but for me it's fun because I'm a professional ...the equipment and the skills. I used to do family portraits at a studio.

MANAGER: Oh, really. I didn't know that.

WHAT JUST HAPPENED: You just put yourself on the list of your company's photographers. This "strength" could come in handy for a stretch assignment or to broaden your network while using it later for the company. Doing new or different things brings you into contact with different people, internally and externally.

Example

MANAGER: Can you proofread this PowerPoint presentation for me, and fix any mistakes in it while you're doing it?

YOU: Yes, I'll do it now. I love working with PowerPoint. Last month, I helped Jenni and Bob create a presentation that they said was awesome. Apparently I have a knack for this type of stuff.

MANAGER: Oh, you helped out on the presentation for the Realtor's Association meeting. I didn't know.

YOU: I did. It was fun. And Bob said the presentation was a big part of why our company got that account. So it was cool that I was able to contribute to that success even though my part was behind the scenes.

MANAGER: Well, accolades to you.

YOU: Thank you. Let me get on this PowerPoint for you now.

WHAT JUST HAPPENED: You told your manager or executive about your accomplishment that contributed to company results. Otherwise, he may not have known (unless you also spoke about it during your periodic performance appraisal session).

Make your self-promotion comments memorable.

Telling something as a story, or in anecdote form, is often memorable. But don't overuse this format. Too much of any one format is overkill and monotonous.

Example

MANAGER: Have you been to one of these conferences before? Working it or sitting in on it?

YOU: Oh, yea. Can I tell you a quick story about how I became an 'accidental speaker' at the ABC conference – in front of 500 people?

MANAGER: You spoke on stage? Tell me more.

YOU: I did. What happened was [executive Sally's assistant] Daria came down with Laryngitis, and she was supposed to introduce Sally on stage in a couple of hours. Daria could still speak but she sounded hoarse; Sally told her, "You sound like the mobster from xyz movie," and I was chuckling about that because it was true and it was funny.

Then Sally said, "No way. Switch assignments with Sue." And I wasn't chuckling anymore. I was in shock. I was thinking, "Oh my goodness; she wants me to be a first-time speaker in front of 500 people." By the time I finished my nightmare, Sally was gone and so I couldn't back out. So I did it. And I survived. Daria said I was a pretty good speaker. Who knew!

WHAT JUST HAPPENED: You wove a story into a conversation about an accomplishment, a new skill, and your potential for taking on a new responsibility. Your manager now will be thinking you can do more than just hand out name tags at the conference entryway.

Keep your comments interesting or entertaining.

Consciously pay attention to nonverbal motions and reactions of the person with whom you are speaking to determine reception of your comments. Is your listener leaning in, "all ears," or stepping backward with one foot and losing eye contact with you? The first means, "That's interesting." The second stance means you are making that person uncomfortable; she either doesn't like the topic or truly needs to break away for another engagement. Take this responsiveness of your audience into account and adjust your conversation appropriately.

For instance, if the other person's body language is indicating she'd rather not hear more, then you should smoothly change the conversation. You're not interesting or entertaining in this case, or perhaps the topic is awkward. Therefore, you want to avoid making that person more uncomfortable or causing an awkward moment. That's not tooting your own horn well.

If you lack transitional communication skills to get out of the conversation you started, just use a straight-forward, lighthearted statement: "Well, I think I've digressed into telling you more than you need to know or hear on that topic. Let's move onto subject x." Then immediately do so.

If it appears to be a case of the other person seems busy or in a hurry, then stop and say: "You know, I just realized I'm rambling on without thought to what you were doing. I'll fill you in on this story another time because I don't want to keep you from preparing for your next appointment."

How will you know if someone is busy or in a hurry? If the person doesn't tell you, watch for body language. For instance, the person looks toward her watch or the clock on the desk, or she looks at a piece of paper in her hand while you're talking. That means something else has her attention, not you. Therefore, that's not a good time for self-promotion. Good timing is important when it comes to self-promotion in the workplace or at related events. Timing can affect receptiveness of your words by the person with whom you are speaking.

On the other hand, maybe your self-promotion comments are interesting or entertaining. You know this because the other person is leaning in like a kid listening to a good bedtime story. Use this experience to repeat this modus operandi in the future. Of course, use a different self-promotion story each time for the same person. You can repeat a story for a different person.

But don't overdo it in frequency. Choose your self-promotion tactics, timing and frequency wisely. A little of the right words and stories can go a long way, especially spoken to the right people (depending on the results you're looking for from your self-promotion).

Keep your self-promotion comments relevant.

That means if you're in a staff meeting in which part of the team is discussing their upcoming business trip to China, and you have been to China, speak up. Say, "I want to chime in here that I've been to China, so I know a little bit about a little bit if you need help with cultural codes or making travel reservations and getting around there."

Irrelevant would be chiming in with, "Oh, China. Take me as your assistant on that trip," or "Oh, China, my mother visited there last year; she loved the place."

Self-promotion should make you look good, not ditzy. You're doing the self-promotion to get results that help your administrative role and career. So choose your comments wisely or don't comment at all.

Don't constantly self-promote.

Have a strategy for self-promotion that leads to intended results for you. Use these communication strategies to self-promote when they serve that goal. For example, you want to become known as the expert in some area so you can broaden your responsibilities in the company for a potential lateral move in the future. Or you want to keep your busy manager informed enough to always remember your value to the department and company. Or you want to let people on a committee know that you have the experience and skills required to be on it; that way perhaps you'll be considered for the committee when new members are sought next year.

There are more communication strategies for self-promoting (verbally and in writing) and more reasons for doing it that are valid reasons. Think about it. Self-promotion is part of your administrative career strategy. And it can benefit those on the receiving end too as noted in some of the examples above. If you don't tell people about you and what you've done and potentially can do, no one else will do so most of the time. How would they know? You've got to tell them!

Plus everyone else is busy; they don't always have time to take note of what you're doing or have done, and give you a pat on the back or recognize what it means in terms of what you can do. Sometimes people in your own company (including your manager or executive) don't understand the significance or scope of what you've done any more than you might understand some achievement the guy in the IT department is raving about when he says he just "killed a big bug."

Therefore, you've got to communicate, using specific communication strategies, what you've done and your accomplishments. You've got to communicate this in ways that others can understand and that perhaps explains some relevance to them. Give those people an "aha moment:" "Oh, really. You've done that. Well, you need to be on our xyz committee next year." Or they think and say: "Oh, you can do that! Wow. We didn't know. We need your help then with preparing this account presentation."

You can't solely rely on other people to pass on the good word about your achievements to your manager. You can't rely on other people to pass on the word about your achievements to those who would benefit, or would benefit you, by knowing this information. Third parties at work are not your personal or professional publicity team. You don't have one. You're it!

You must get the self-promotion messages out that you want heard and that you want to emphasize about you. When you rely on other people to be your spokespersons, you're also relying on them to choose the messages they share about you. Therefore, they define your accomplishments and personal brand. The better way is for you to take control of your own self-promotion. That way you strategically deliver the messages of importance to you about you. You define your personal brand overall in the workplace.

Put it in a Portfolio

Another way to remember and strategically communicate all you do is to "show, don't tell." You do this by showcasing your accomplishments and capabilities for current and potential employers in what is called a professional portfolio. That's a digital and/or physical object (e.g. binder) in which you put examples and samples of your work and accomplishments. You could use the portfolio during performance reviews or other meetings with your current employer where the portfolio supports and facilitates your meeting purpose.

For example, maybe you want to "show" (not just "tell") your manager that you can stretch your job responsibilities to take on desktop publishing for the department. Your portfolio contains the "proof" that you can do what you say you can do. You put samples of your desktop publishing achievements in your portfolio. You put any certificates you've earned for software program proficiency or classes related to desktop publishing tools in it. Bring a customized version of the portfolio to the meeting with your manager in which you plan to broach this topic.

What's meant by *customized* is you keep two portfolios. The first is a master portfolio for your eyes only at home. It contains everything you can think of to put in your professional portfolio (also sometimes referred to as a *career portfolio*). The second portfolio is flexible and customized as needed per situation in which you'll be showing it. You copy items from the master portfolio to the one you're customizing for your particular needs.

A particular need could be as mentioned above that you want to showcase your desktop publishing abilities in order to explain your strength and interest in expanding that part of your job. Or perhaps you are preparing a portfolio for a job interview at a company in which you want to communicate certain accomplishments and skills, but not your entire career life (thus the customized portfolio and not the master portfolio). Or maybe it's time for your performance appraisal session and you want to communicate to your manager some of your achievements from this past year. Show, not just tell, with the use of the portfolio.

A professional portfolio is a communication strategy that is nonverbal, though you can certainly narrate what you're showcasing. It depends on the situation. If you are giving it to your manager to browse before the performance appraisal, no words needed; just add a note that you're giving him some prep items for the upcoming performance review session. If you're showing it to a prospective employer during a job interview, you might want to briefly mention what he's looking at per page; point out a few highlights. Don't talk nonstop though. Give him some quiet time to absorb the portfolio's contents too.

Your professional portfolio can be on paper or digital or both. It is a communication tool. Use it as part of your communication strategy for communicating your accomplishments and abilities. Make sure the portfolio represents you well in regard to contents and clarity and overall presentation. It's part of your personal brand. Read a list of some potential items to put in your career portfolio in Appendix C.

***

Chapter 3 Recap:

- Your accomplishments can often be thought of as results, even goals at times; employers like results.
- The ability to communicate your workplace results will help you in your administrative career, such as when seeking broader responsibility, new assignments, promotions, and increases in salary.
- Communicating accomplishments enables you to distinctly represent yourself and the administrative position as more than a so-called "overhead expense." You connect the dots for employers to clearly see your value and that of your role.
- You need to learn to recognize your accomplishments and results because they do exist in your administrative role.
- Sometimes you need to self-promote about your accomplishments, expertise and value in the workplace.
- Self-promotion is not bragging; it's a way to communicate what you've done. It's important for various reasons to communicate about what you've done.
- Don't wait on others in your company to endorse you. Learn communication strategies for discussing what you've done: your accomplishments and results.
- Sometimes daily administrative tasks you do can be *bundled* into accomplishments and results.
- Keep ongoing documentation in your own personal folder of your accomplishments. Don't rely on your memory.

- Verbal self-promotion by you can occur anywhere – during conversations in the hallway or in official performance review sessions. *When* and *where* is less important than the *how* to do it and *how long* to do it.

- Keep your self-promotion comments short, memorable, interesting or entertaining and relevant. However, don't constantly self-promote; use this communication strategy with deliberation.

- Self-promotion should always be part of your administrative career strategy. While it benefits you, it also benefits those on the receiving end more than you might think. For instance, managers learn about you and what you've done and potentially can do for them.

- Another way to remember and strategically communicate all you do is to "show, don't tell" by showcasing your accomplishments and capabilities for current and potential employers in what is called a professional portfolio (career portfolio).

- Keep a master career portfolio and break it down into a customized portfolio pending the situation for which you are using it. Your professional portfolio can be on paper or digital or both.

- A professional portfolio is a communication strategy that is nonverbal, though you can certainly narrate what you're showcasing.

Chapter 4

Communicating What You Can Do

Your manager or executive knows you're capable of certain work assignments. This is because when he interviewed you for the job, together you both discussed the knowledge and skills needed to do those types of tasks or projects. You had those skills or that knowledge, and still do. That's why your manager or executive hired you – so you could use that knowledge and skills toward his benefit and that of the company.

What your manager or executive doesn't know is what else you can do. That job interview didn't cover your entire life and work history. Likewise, your manager is not maintaining a journal of everything new you've been learning ongoing since you started working for him. You may have learned things on your own on the job or outside of working hours. And this is where you come in and start communicating. You tell your manager or executive what you can do as appropriate and useful to you or him.

This is especially important if you're feeling underutilized. Some administrative professionals do feel that way. It's also important to communicate what you can do if you want more challenging work. If that's you, you're not alone there either. Plenty of administrative professionals want more work or broader assignments and responsibilities. Sometimes the only way to get that is to ask for it. You'll need a communication strategy for that!

Give Me More

The meaning of the phrases "Give me more assignments or broader responsibilities" and "I can do that for you" aren't all that much different in concept when communicated strategically. To do this, just observe what you're passing on to your manager and offer to take it back: "I always give you callers asking questions about xyz. I've listened and learned from your responses to those callers so much through the years that I believe I can answer such questions directly now. Would you like me to do so instead of passing them to you each time?"

You can use that strategic phrasing with a little tweaking for similar requests: "I've been proofreading these status reports for you for more than a year now, and I've become familiar with their composition. I could give you some of your time back by drafting them for you. Do you want to try me out on that?"

Notice you're not saying "I'm bored" or "I'm not challenged" even though you're solving that problem too (if it's a problem for you). Instead you're communicating specific instances where you can help your manager or executive. Simultaneously you're asking for more responsibility and work without explicitly and generally stating that. It's a clever communication strategy to communicate and ask for what you can do (and want to do).

It's also noteworthy phrasing (in the examples above) because you're being specific. You could have been nonspecific and simply asked your manager or executive for more to do in general: "Is there more I can do for you?"

However, that's not a very effective communication strategy (if it's one at all) because you're putting your manager on the spot, and he may have no idea what more to give you to do. He also may not know all you can do for him. If your manager does come up with something more for you to do, it may be something you don't want to do or that's really not maximizing your assistance for him. Nonspecific requests like that get you nonspecific results. If you are utilizing a communication strategy, you will make a specific request intended to get a specific result. No surprises there; just good communication strategy.

Hey, I Can do That for You

Oddly, getting your managers and executives or others you support to delegate to you sometimes takes effort (and clever communication strategies). You'd think it would be easy all of the time because you'd think managers would want to give you more work in order to get more work done overall in the workplace. You ask, they give, right? Plus, you'd think delegation would be a manager's strong suit. Not so. A lot of people in positions you report to aren't good at "letting go" of tasks. Maybe they like doing some of the tasks too. Or perhaps they're not comfortable just giving you a desired outcome and saying make it happen. These executives and managers stay too involved with the work, or do it themselves. And that's a waste of a good assistant – and that manager's time.

The reason some managers or executives might lack this ability to delegate and let you do things you can do for them could be for various reasons. It may be that you have a young manager or executive new to his role overall. He's not delegating to you because he doesn't know how to utilize an administrative professional. He's never had an assistant before. Perhaps he's never had a management position either.

Or maybe your manager or executive doesn't trust you – not because of anything you've done but because he's been "burned" by some bad assistance in the past. Your manager learned it was better not to delegate more than absolutely necessary and even then to micromanage the delegation.

Then again, some managers or executives are micromanagers by nature, with perfectionist tendencies. You sure can do whatever it is, but your manager has a hard time believing you can do it the same or better – at least not without detailed directions and constant oversight. Ugh!

Another reason for lack of delegation is your manager may not be aware of all or any of your strengths (spoken more about in the next section). You can do something for him, and do it well, but he has no idea that you can do that. Or maybe your manager does know about your strength but doesn't realize it can be applied to certain administrative tasks or parts of projects he's currently doing solo. You'll have to connect the dots in that case for your manager.

Finally, some managers just don't see the value in letting go of a task or project. What's in it for him to turn over control of a certain task or project to you when he can do it just fine too?

It's important to give thought to some of those reasons and determine whether or not they match your situation with your manager or executive. That way you can use the right communication strategy with that person to say: "Hey, I can do that for you. Really!"

For instance, take the last scenario of your executive doing a task himself. Maybe he's in his office right now typing away in PowerPoint software. He's creating a presentation that he could have given you his notes for and said, "Create a draft PowerPoint slide presentation from this highlighted material." So why is he doing it himself? Well, he knows what he wants and thinks he can do it quicker, and he enjoys using PowerPoint.

You'll have to step up and step in to get this assignment. This is work for an assistant. Trust me, *his* manager is not seeing value in paying him a managerial or executive salary to create his own PowerPoint presentations.

Say: "I'm good with PowerPoint. I use it all the time and so don't have a learning curve on the features. I can create your PowerPoint presentation for you from scratch just off of your notes you give me for the content and a short description of any special bells and whistles you want me to include."

Pending your particular situation and manager, you could add: "Then you can use your time to do the bigger picture management [or executive] stuff until I have a first draft ready. I can do this for you if you delegate it to me."

If necessary, further explain that the more your manager lets go and delegates to you, the more you both will become in synch with what he wants and his style. With time, your assistance on tasks and projects using this new knowledge will gain your manager even more time to work on "other stuff;" you'll handle what he's doing now himself. So investing more time now in delegation can have bigger long-term rewards and benefits for both of you.

Another lack of delegation instance mentioned above was attributed to a manager who's never had an assistant. So it's time for you to train that manager. Say: "Let's sit down over coffee and meet to talk about all the things I can do for you as your assistant because some you might not know about. I can be a valuable resource in freeing up your time and helping you get things done. I want to let you know how you can better utilize my role on your behalf."

Then there was the situation where your manager perhaps just doesn't trust you and your capabilities due to his past experiences, not due to your current experience. Talk about this without talking about those particular bad assistant experiences by working phrasing like this into an appropriate conversation:

Example

ADMIN: Sometimes you may have tasks or goals that you're hesitant to completely delegate to me because you're not sure yet I can do or fulfill them on my own. So what I'd like to do is start making my results for you more transparent, maybe by having a daily meeting or giving you daily status reports to keep you informed of what I'm doing. That way you'll see what I can do. Are you open to that?

MANAGER: Yes, tell me more.

ADMIN: I'm thinking that then as we work more together, we'll grow more in synch and you can feel more comfortable offloading more of your projects and goals to me. I know I can do them, but I want *you* to be comfortable in knowing that too. So I'm going to schedule 10 minute status meetings for us three times a week in the mornings. And I'm going to e-mail you a short daily status update at the end of each work day. How does that sound to you?

MANAGER: I like the idea. Let's try it.

Use your own words. Pause to let your manager or executive join in the conversation. But you can use the general concepts of the phrasing above. Guide the conversation to the results you need with your communication strategy.

Again, you first want to define the root "problem:" why your manager or executive doesn't delegate what you can do to you. Once you know that root cause, then you can work on finding the right communication strategy to convey "Hey, I can do that for you" based on that specific root cause.

Finding the root cause may take observation, a few strategic questions and even some background research along with analytical thinking to determine that root cause. You can't just say: "Hey, what's wrong with you? Why don't you delegate more to me because I can do those things for you?" Do your background research, plan your communication strategy and implement it.

Highlight Your Strengths

What do you do well? It could be writing, speaking, using software, doing math, and/or planning events. It could be even less direct skills and tasks like shopping for bargains, mingling with people and making small talk, or leaving customers feeling attended to and like their needs were met (even when you just gave them a "don't know yet" status update).

You may, and likely do, have several strengths that you use, or can use, at work. Assess your potential strengths. Some of your attributes or capabilities may be so ordinary or routine to you that you don't even realize they would be considered strengths in someone else's view. Make a list of strengths and potential strengths. Review the list ongoing. Add to the list ongoing.

Then communicate those strengths ongoing as appropriate to those you support such as by saying, "I'm good at *this*, and therefore I can do *that* for you if you'll delegate it to me because of this strong point I have."

That's all you have to say to get the conversation flowing: "Hey, I can do that for you, and here's why I can do it for you. It's one of my strengths to do xyz."

If your forte is computers and software, offer to conduct training and orientation sessions related to that. Offer to make helpful spreadsheets and to format and design reports for your manager. Let your manager or executive know you can help with specific computer and software related tasks and projects. Be known as the expert in that area.

If you're a good writer, offer to be a second set of eyes for proofreading and minor editing. Suggest that you draft correspondence or company Blog articles on behalf of your manager or executive. Let your manager know you can draft his bio for brochures or help write white papers on his behalf.

If you're good at speaking in front of crowds, tell your manager you'd be happy to introduce him any time necessary at conferences where your manager is presenting. Let him know you can present segments in all-hands meetings or other type meetings where he would like help.

If you're good with running meetings and keeping people focused and on schedule, tell your manager or executive that you'll be happy to be a facilitator, or co-facilitator to him, as needed at his workshops. Offer to play a bigger role with coordinating meetings and special events. Let him know you can handle any task that involves heavy scheduling skills.

If you're a successful bargain shopper and negotiator when shopping, offer to handle purchases of office furnishings, equipment and supplies. Mention it's your forte to get good deals on a limited budget. Say you can handle details and negotiating for meeting room rentals or event space.

Focus on capitalizing on your strengths. Ask for more of what you're already good at doing. Also apply your strengths to parts of projects and support roles you're not yet doing but for which your strengths make you qualified (see the brainstorming your strengths table in Appendix D). Your personal brand is in your strengths. It's nice to improve on weaknesses as needed, but your time is limited in the workplace and in your career overall. It's a better use of your time to point out and focus on doing more of what you're good at versus what you're not so good at.

The exception is when you must do something at work and your lack of skills will affect the outcome negatively. Then it's a good use of your time to refine that weak skill or learn it. Otherwise, highlight your strengths in communication (and action) to make the point of what you can do in the workplace. This will result in you attaining more accomplishments in the workplace and a positive reputation. Naturally, this also results in your doing more helpful things for your manager or executive and company. It's a win-win scenario for all involved when you focus on further utilizing and highlighting your strengths in the workplace.

Doing Stretch Goals

Sometimes you hear the term "stretch goal" when asked to set workplace goals. It simply means stretching – reaching – to do something that's a bit of a challenge for you. Put emphasis on the "bit of a challenge." It is improper to create an excessive "stretch" to complete the goal. That would be an "almost impossible" goal, not a "stretch goal." A stretch goal should be challenging but still achievable and within your reach.

For instance, you set a goal to create and maintain an office supplies budget, which your office currently doesn't have. You've never created a budget. However, you're familiar with reading budgets. You also currently purchase office supplies and maintain inventory for the department. Therefore creating an office supplies budget is a stretch for you but not impossible. You *can* do this.

You don't have to be asked to set a stretch goal to want to do so. You can set stretch goals whenever you want to. And you can use stretch goals to say, "I can do that for you." Here's how:

If you have a strength, as mentioned in the above section, ask to do a stretch goal based off of it. So in essence, perhaps you're not explicitly saying you actually *can* do that (as in for certain capabilities), but you're saying: "I'd like to do that [task, project, or assignment]. I haven't actually done it before but I have suitable strengths [or knowledge] to do it, and it would be a fun challenge – sort of a stretch goal for me. Can I do it for you, with your input as needed, of course?"

Quite often your manager or executive will say yes to such a phrased request, which is the response you're seeking. For some simple tips on how to more formally set a workplace goal, see the SMART goals formula in Appendix E.

***

Chapter 4 Recap:

- Your manager is not maintaining a journal of everything new you've been learning ongoing since you started working for him. You've got to tell him what you can do as appropriate and useful to you or him.
- If you feel underutilized or want more challenging work, communicate to your manager or executive about what you can do. Be specific in asking for certain assignments.
- Use the technique of observing what you're passing on to your manager and offer to take it back to maximize or free up his time.
- You'd think delegation would be a strong suit for a manager or executive, but that's not always the case. This is for many reasons including the executive likes doing the task or she doesn't know how to best (if at all) utilize an assistant.
- Non-delegation by managers and executives is a waste of their time at work and of your assistance.
- It's important to give thought to the reason your manager or executive doesn't delegate more to you so you can use the right communication strategy to say: "Hey, I can do that for you. Really!"
- A strength is something you do well, and you likely have several strengths that you use or can use at work. Assess your strengths ongoing.
- Communicate your strengths ongoing to those you support to help them understand that you can do something in particular for them if they delegate it.

- Focus on capitalizing on your strengths, not your weaknesses. Point out your strengths, not your weaknesses. Your personal brand is in your strengths as is your increased potential assistance and value to your manager or executive.
- Only worry about your weaknesses when you must do something at work and your lack of skills will affect the outcome negatively.
- A stretch goal is when you reach to do something that is achievable but a bit of a challenge for you.
- If you have a strength, ask to do a stretch goal based off of it – something you haven't actually done but that your strengths give you the capability to do. Use this as a way to say, "I can do that for you."

Chapter 5

Communicating What You Can't Do

You're "super admin" – so you can do everything, right? Maybe so if you're looking for the quickest route to job and career burnout. In that case, sure you can do everything – just for a very short while.

However, the authentic administrative professional knows her capabilities and her limitations. She learns and makes notes of how long it takes her to do certain types of tasks and projects for future reference when doing the same types of work. She asks questions about the scope of each project handed to her. She takes into account time out for interruptions, stretch and stress-relief breaks, and lunch (food for energy is important) and builds that into suggested deadlines.

She speaks up (and with potential solutions) when the workload is burying her. She lets those she supports know when she can't meet their suggested deadlines. She does not disappoint her customers because she sets accurate expectations for them in her efforts to support them and deliver the goods. So how does this administrative professional communicate what she "can't" do? How will you do so? It's done with communication strategies like these that you too can emulate:

Explain "Work Overload" Without Complaining

When discussing your seemingly excessive workload with your manager or executive, your word choices matter. The wrong words could easily make you sound whiny and like a complainer. Therefore, when broaching the subject of work overload, don't focus on you; instead, focus on work outcomes and concerns related to those outcomes. Explain how the outcome of a particular work-overload dilemma could or will affect your company or manager's positive expectations for something or in some way. Then try to immediately suggest a solution. By doing that, you'll be seen as someone with foresight and initiative who also is a problem solver, rather than potentially as a complainer or whiny individual who's not pulling his or her share in the office.

Here's an example of bringing attention to your hefty workload and consequences in a way that's not whiny. Rather it is solution-oriented while saving your executive from undesirable consequences of what is essentially your work-overload issue.

Example

YOU: Hi there [manager]. I need a minute to run something by you.

MANAGER: Okay, I got a minute. Go.

YOU: It's about the weekly reports you take to the director's meeting. I'm creating three of them now due every Tuesday by 5 p.m., and I only get the input for them all by late Monday. That's fine, and I like doing them.

I have a concern though. It's that I might make a mistake while rushing to get them all done on time. I do not want to embarrass us both in the director's meeting with invalid data. I need time to thoroughly proofread them before giving them to you. And time is the issue or solution here depending on how you look at it. Can we discuss shifting some of my other Tuesday assignments and tasks elsewhere so I can focus entirely on just preparing these reports every Tuesday?

MANAGER: Absolutely. You're right to be concerned. The director loves his reports and accuracy is important. One turned into three pretty quickly, but it's all good stuff you've been giving us. We use the data every meeting. So let's discuss what else you're doing on Tuesdays so we can make more time for you to work on them.

YOU: Okay. I made a list, so I'll give you a quick overview of what's on it, and then we can go back over each one.

Your issue and consequences may differ. Regardless, you can use the same format to discuss your work overload issue in terms of preventing unwanted consequences to your manager, executive, company, clients, or coworkers. It's about the outcome, the quality of the product or service, the risk to your company, the inconvenience to your company's customers, how it will reflect on your manager or executive, etc., not you. At least that's the way you should phrase this type of dilemma when you can do so.

Save the day and save yourself from work overload and potential workplace burnout with this communication strategy. You are conveying real consequences too, not just something you're strategically inventing. So you can feel good about communicating in this manner. You're just changing the perception of the problem (i.e. work overload in this case). You move from the focus solely on you and what you can't do to the focus on what else could happen and what you can do about it proactively to prevent it.

Negotiating Impossible Deadlines

You may immediately recognize when you're given an assignment that you're unlikely to meet the suggested deadline. The reason might be that it's an unrealistic timeframe for the amount and quality of work requested. Or perhaps it would be a reasonable timeframe if you had nothing else on your plate that shared the same deadline and schedule.

Also, sometimes as an administrative professional, you may take on more work than you can handle. You do this because you don't want to disappoint anyone you support or seem less accomplished than you actually are. Or you say "yes" to all assignments and deadlines because you think it's required of you. Isn't it part of the administrative job description to do what your manager tells you without question or comment?

No! That's a false assumption. Managers and executives don't want bad surprises: "Whoops – it's 4 o'clock. I missed your deadline. You want it halfway done like this, or should I keep working on it?"

Managers and executives want you to alert them as soon as you realize that you have conflicting or unrealistic deadlines. You are the expert in administrative matters and assignments, not them. Use that expertise to let managers and executives know the amount of time you think it will take you to accomplish an administrative project (anticipating some interruptions). Suggest a different timeline to your manager based on your calculations. If there is someone your manager can delegate part of the work to in order to meet the original deadline, suggest this as part of the solution too.

Negotiating timelines is about keeping your manager or executive informed about what you can do and can't do while working together to reset the timeline. No heavy negotiating skills are needed. Just have a conversation. Communicate strategically.

Example

YOU: I understand you need this by 4 p.m. today, but I don't want to stay silent and mislead you into thinking that I can accomplish that in two hours. It's going to take me a little longer.

MANAGER: How much longer do you think?

YOU: Based on what you've just told me needs to be done and my experience doing this type of work, it's likely going to take me three or four hours.

MANAGER: That long. I didn't realize.

YOU: Yes, that's my estimate and I'm pretty efficient at this type of stuff. But I know a possible way to speed things up. If you can ask Mary to help me by having her doing x while I do y, then that would probably cut the timeline down by an hour, maybe a little more. Then I can have the completed job to you by about 4:30.

MANAGER: Okay. Go ahead and start while I ask her about it and send her over if she can.

Below is another example of phrasing for negotiation of work assignment timelines.

Example

YOU: So you need it be 4 p.m.?

MANAGER: Yes, 4 o'clock is when I'd like it.

YOU: Uh, oh, ... normally I could do that in that timeframe, but I can't get away from the desk right now to do parts of it that need to be done elsewhere because I'm handling the phone lines. We're expecting a bunch of phone-in RSVPs today for the PSP Conference. Are you flexible with that 4 p.m. deadline?

MANAGER: Well, actually, yes, I can be. When do you think you can complete it?

YOU: I can do parts A, B and C here and now in between answering the phone. And I can pick up the D and E parts after 5 p.m. on the way home. I'd have them with me when I come in at 8 a.m. tomorrow and then could have the whole thing ready for you at 9 a.m. Is that okay?

MANAGER: That'll work. Thank you for letting me know what you can do. I've got to go out now, but I'll see you at 9 a.m. tomorrow to pick them up on the way to the meeting. Thank you.

If your manager stands firm with the deadline (vs. renegotiating it) and says the useless adage, "Just do the best you can," at the very least you've informed him or her. Your manager or executive won't be surprised if you miss the original deadline.

But likely your manager or executive will negotiate a new timeline with you or other solution. This will especially happen after you've built up trust and credibility in your business relationship with your manager or executive and in your administrative performance and expertise. Until then, you may have to speak up to renegotiate deadlines but also to explain in further detail why a deadline isn't feasible. Your manager may not understand the complexity of a matter he delegates to you in addition to any conflicting deadlines or other issues. Strategically communicate this information. You are the administrative expert!

Discussing Your Weaknesses

You've got weaknesses in your workplace skills. Everyone has them, including your managers and executives. It's how you convey them that counts. For instance, picture this conversation scenario between an administrative professional and her executive:

ADMIN: You want me to do what! Take minutes at the Board Meeting next month. What? Every month? Okay, just one question: "What are minutes, and how do you take them?" Well, I guess that's really two questions.

EXECUTIVE: So I'm guessing minute-taking is not one of your strengths.

ADMIN: Bingo!

Wow! That was an uncomfortable conversation. You might want to tone it down a little bit. Also, explain to your manager or executive that while you have many administrative strengths, you have some weaknesses too. Let's play that conversation again with a new spin on the dialogue:

ADMIN: So you need me to take minutes at the Board Meetings starting next month onward?

EXECUTIVE: Yes, is that okay?

ADMIN: Of course. I just need to prepare before the first meeting because I've never taken minutes. I'm going to look for a resource like a Webinar or book on minute taking so I can get the lowdown on how to do it right. Can I charge that resource to the company?

EXECUTIVE: Yes, just keep the cost for the resources under $200 or run it by me first if it's more.

ADMIN: Okay. I'll need to meet with you too prior to the first meeting. In order to take good minutes, I need to know about what goes on at the board meetings and the process, terminology, who's who and any expectations you have for the format of the minutes. I'll schedule that meeting on your calendar.

EXECUTIVE: Sounds like a plan. Do it. Thank you. I'm off to my next meeting now. I'll be back sometime after 2 o'clock.

It's always smart to highlight and work on doing more of what you're good at: your strengths. Incorporate your strengths into potential new assignments and responsibilities. But realize that even though you don't spend your time announcing to your employer and others what you're not good at or can't do (your weaknesses), that sometimes incorporating one of your weaker areas into your administrative job and role will be necessary.

When that happens, just communicate honestly with your manager or executive that [fill in the blank] is not your forte. Or simply say, "I've never done that before," or "I don't have that skill – yet [with emphasis on 'yet']." Then follow that phrase with some positive phrasing about how you plan to become stronger in that area, and ask for any help or resources you need to make it happen. That's a reasonable plan to communicate "what you can't do" with a positive and practical spin on the dialogue.

That's what your manager or executive wants to hear anyway. Your manager may at times expect you to perform magic and "pull a rabbit out of a hat." That is because so many times the administrative professional seems to somehow do that, especially the more experienced ones. So it just starts to become natural for executives to throw new challenges and needs at you without actually thinking through if and how you can do it. Your managers or executives don't necessarily know how to do what they've asked, and they don't always know if you know how to do it or can do it either. They just know you've seemingly done magic in the past for them. So they ask you to do it.

But when you're out of tricks, your manager or executive expects you to just flat out tell him: "Hold up there. No magic or miracle is going to enable me to pull that assignment off for you. I just don't have the skill to do it. But I can get it [like this] and then do that for you all year long."

Busy managers and executives don't have time to guess at your weaknesses when they need you to incorporate one into an assignment for them. They just need to know how you're going to accomplish the assignment (and often they don't even need that part) and the timeline for the expected results. Don't put on a show when you can't do something; be forthright and be ready to strengthen this weakness quickly. Or be ready to find someone who can help you out on short notice – the benefits of relationship building and a good network.

***

Chapter 5 Recap:
- Trying to do everything in your administrative role is a sure path to job and career burnout. You can't do everything at once or all of the time.
- Communicate to your managers and executives what you can't do as appropriate and relevant.
- You can explain "work overload" without complaining by focusing on concerns related to outcomes of the relevant assignments rather than focusing on its effect on you.
- Bring solutions to your manager when you bring concerns related to work overload issues. You'll be viewed as someone with foresight and initiative who is a problem solver.
- When you convey consequences of work overload, you are being honest. The communication strategy is that you're changing the perception of the problem from one focused solely on you to potential consequences to others or the company.

- Alert managers when you have conflicting or unrealistic deadlines.

- Learn how to negotiate impossible deadlines.

- After you have built up trust and credibility in your business relationship with your manager, she will take your word for assignment timelines more often without asking you for more details.

- Managers or executives who delegate work to you may not understand the complexity of a matter. You need to communicate this information so they will understand the scope and timeframes of the work.

- Even though you don't regularly announce your weaknesses, when one arises you should candidly admit to it. Relay a plan for overcoming the weakness and getting the related task or project done.

Chapter 6

Communicating What You Will Do

Managers and executives new to their roles, new to you as their assistant, or new to even having an assistant sometimes get confused about what you will do or they should ask you to do. That's why they may not be utilizing your assistance as much as you think they could be. Or that's why they may be giving you tasks you don't believe you should be doing as an administrative professional. They may even be embarrassed to tell you they are not quite sure what an administrative professional or assistant will do or won't do. Some managers and executives are confused about where they should draw the line in assigning you tasks. Sometimes you can help end this awkwardness and confusion by assertively and tactfully communicating what you will do.

Onboarding a New Manager to Your Assistance

So what do you say to that new manager or executive? You say: "I think as we work together you may find I will do some things to assist you that maybe you don't yet know are tasks and assignments and assistant can or will do. If your need is administrative in nature, even seemingly a bit managerial, ask me. I will do it. That's my role here on this team as the administrative professional."

You might also onboard a new manager by giving him a list of what you will do. Also include examples of some things you've been assigned and done in the past. Don't make it an overwhelming detailed list; a one- or two-page bullet point list will work. When you give it to your manager, use tact and diplomacy:

"We haven't worked together before, so I want to make sure you feel comfortable assigning me tasks that'll be of real assistance to you. I made this list of some things I will be happy to do if you just let me know. This is the short list. I know other things will come up ongoing that I can assist you with too."

You might discuss the list with your manager, perhaps use it as a conversation starter about your role, or just give him the list to look over on his own schedule. Also, if you have a career portfolio (mentioned in chapter 3), then you could leave a customized version of it with your new manager. That way he can see and review on his time what you will do, can do and have done.

When onboarding your manager or executive, you want to set expectations for your upcoming workplace partnership – ones you both agree upon and can fulfill. See the sample new manager onboarding cheat sheet in Appendix F.

Do You Do Coffee?

The administrative professional position has progressed through the years, perhaps into what was once thought of as middle management positions. Yet there is still the dilemma for many managers and executives and their assistants over simple requests such as for making coffee in the office. Managers wonder if it's okay to ask an assistant to make coffee or is that unprofessional or demeaning. Executives wonder will she quit if I ask her to bring me coffee or pick up a working lunch for me. Administrative professionals wonder where it states the ability to make and bring another employee coffee in that business curriculum they studied in school. Surely, coffee making and serving is not an "administrative" task or responsibility.

Indeed it is not. Every administrative professional should maintain professionalism and use assertiveness and common sense in letting his or her manager or executive know where boundaries start and stop. How else will some of them know what you will do for them (or won't). In regard to the coffee dilemma specifically, making or getting coffee *for guests* falls under the realm of the assistant, even one with "administrative" in the title.

It's courtesy. And while your manager or executive may offer to do it himself, it's something you can do to assist him; that way your executive and his guest can get right to their business together. Treat your office guests the way you would expect to be treated if you were the guest in their offices. That's the simple guideline to follow in that type of situation.

As for the willingness to bring your manager or executive coffee (or any other drink or even lunch) as part of your administrative role, that's something you have to work out together (assuming you're an administrative or executive assistant and not a personal assistant). In truth, coffee making and serving is not going to fall very high on the list of priorities of an assistant who is being well utilized. So in many offices such dilemmas of administrative tasks vs. non-administrative tasks or seemingly personal tasks don't happen.

However, there are some assistants – especially to executives – who say those they support can be very busy and running ragged on some days; therefore, bringing them a drink or picking up their lunch while they continue to work is vital to keeping them functioning and on schedule. These assistants also say their executives are usually appreciative; they understand that this type of service isn't necessarily the norm in the role of today's assistants – often referred to as administrative professionals in general.

Specifically, some administrative professionals have titles such as administrative manager, administrative services director, administrative coordinator, administrative specialist, and more titles beyond traditional [fill in the blank] assistant (though that's still seemingly most prominent). Clearly such evolving growth in these titles reflects more focus on managers and executives delegating a broader list of administrative tasks, assignments and responsibilities to today's administrative professionals; that doesn't always leave time to ask for assistance with a non-administrative task even when such help would be helpful.

The key here again in these non-administrative task scenarios is common sense and courtesy – and respect. It is not your responsibility as an administrative professional to serve your superiors beverages and lunch. However, if you are getting yourself a cup of coffee, there is nothing wrong with asking to bring someone else one. Some managers or executives will do the same for their assistants. If you drink coffee and therefore are willing to make it when you come in, say so. If you don't drink coffee and aren't willing to make it, say that too. If you both drink coffee, work it out: "You make the first pot; I'll make the second or clean it at closing time." But if you're being taken advantage of or disrespected, say no (read more on saying no in the next chapter).

Follow this same train of thought when considering if you will or won't do other non-administrative or seemingly personal tasks (e.g. schedule a doctor's appointment for your executive, pick up a gift for a personal occasion, or drop off dry cleaning). Sometimes it makes sense to do the task along with your administrative tasks and sometimes it doesn't. This is particularly so for higher level support in which executives' personal and professional lives and calendars often do mix (even if they'd rather they didn't). Use your own judgment. Communicate what you will do, and discuss what you believe you should not be doing. You are accountable for your own actions and responses. You set the tone for the professional status and regard you are seeking from others.

Above all else, you must be true to yourself in carving out the administrative professional role you want and in living that role. That is the only way you will attain self-satisfaction in your administrative career. And it is *your career*. You're in charge of it! Use communication strategies prominently in your role and career to shape it how you want it to be.

***

Chapter 6 Recap:

- For various reasons, some managers and executives may not know what you will do as their assistant or where they should draw the line in asking you to do tasks. You can help end this awkwardness and confusion by tactfully and strategically communicating what you will do.

- You may need and want to be proactive about onboarding, or orienting, new managers and executives to things you will do to assist them. There are some things that maybe they don't yet know are tasks and assignments and administrative professional can or will do (or that you in particular can or will do).

- Give a new manager a list of what you will do, and also include examples of some things you've been assigned and done in the past.

- When onboarding your manager or executive, you want to set expectations for your upcoming workplace partnership – ones you both agree upon and can fulfill.

- Use assertiveness and common sense in letting your manager or executive know where boundaries start and stop with their non-administrative requests and task assignments, if any.

- Making and serving coffee is not an administrative task. Making or obtaining coffee for guests of your manager or executive does fall to the assistant.

- Use common sense and courtesy with serving guests. Treat your office guests the way you would expect to be treated if you were the guest in their offices.

- If you want to bring your manager or executive a drink or even a working lunch to help him stay on schedule, that's okay. If you're serving a manager or executive who is capable, not working and has the time to get his own lunch and coffee, assert your opinion about this task.

- As today's assistants are becoming more like what was once considered middle management, the dilemmas of taking on, or objecting to, non-administrative tasks or seemingly personal tasks are becoming less prominent.

- If you are a personal assistant (vs. an executive assistant or administrative assistant), expect to also do personal, non-administrative tasks for your employer (as well as administrative tasks).

- The key to handling non-administrative task scenarios, or dilemmas, is common sense and courtesy – and respect.

- Communicate what you will do, and discuss what you believe you should not be doing. You are accountable for your own actions and responses, and you set the tone for the professional status and regard you are seeking from others.

- Shape your administrative roles and career the way you want. No matter what anybody asks you to do or says to you, it's your career. Take charge of it. Accept accountability.

Chapter 7

Communicating What You Won't Do

Administrative professionals work in a service capacity. You provide assistance to managers, executives or others you support. You want to help people. It's your nature. It's your job. It's the essence of your profession. While doing that, it's important that you don't lose yourself in serving others.

Therefore, you must define your ethics, and decline to do anything unethical. If you don't stand up for yourself, nobody else will; obviously not the person asking you to do something unethical.

Also, you must define your personal and professional boundaries. Keep personal boundaries to help maintain your life which includes work but is not solely defined by your work. Maintain professional boundaries in the workplace and teach others, perhaps gently if possible, not to cross your professional boundaries.

And equally important, learn to say *no* to what you won't do. There are gentle ways to say no when you need to respond in such a way in delicate situations (such as to your manager at times or out of consideration for certain people's feelings). In many cases, saying no directly is fine too. *No* is not a bad word. Really! It's not a "positive" word, but it's not a bad word. Sometimes a direct no may be appropriate. So let's get to the specifics of these communication scenarios and communication strategies starting with ethics.

You Won't do Anything Unethical

In general, the dictionary defines ethics as "a discipline dealing with good and evil and with moral duty; moral principles or practice." It does not separate "personal" ethics from "workplace" ethics, and one would think that they should not be separated and that ethics in your personal life or workplace is a black and white issue, not a gray one. In many cases it is. But is it in every instance?

If only "every" ethical dilemma at work were a clear "yes, I'll do this" and "no, I won't do that," then a lot of stressful situations at work wouldn't happen.

Unfortunately, administrative professionals are not immune to encountering situations in the workplace that test their personal or workplace ethics (if you see any separation between the two).

The tricky part sometimes is three-fold: 1) recognizing ethical dilemmas; 2) deciding or just coming to terms with where you stand on a possible ethical issue; and 3) then knowing how to resolve an ethical dilemma appropriately and to your satisfaction (because it is *your* ethics we're talking about, not the other person's ethics).

Your Ethics in the Workplace

At work, just like at home, you want to and must maintain your personal value system and sometimes that of your employer. However, two people at work don't always have to agree on a certain "value." It's okay to recognize that two people can have different value systems and can still work side by side. But you want to set and enforce your personal ethical boundaries even at work.

That's not always easy. Yet, sometimes it's necessary to keep you out of legal trouble as well as to maintain your personal moral standards and peace-of-mind, which enables you to feel comfortable every day with your work performance. You will not feel proud when you feel you have allowed yourself to be manipulated across a personal ethical boundary. On the other hand, you don't want to turn every assignment and occurrence at work into your personal soap box of *your* ethical standards.

Ethical issues in the workplace for an administrative professional can rank minor to major. You rank them and decide when you must take action to maintain your ethics or enforce a moral boundary important to you.

What are some examples?

How about an administrative professional who is asked to answer the company phone lines with "Merry Christmas" when she prefers "Happy Holidays" due to different beliefs in faith. What would you do in that instance?

Or perhaps your company quality standards have declined. You are starting to feel uncomfortable reassuring callers that their issues will be handled or that the product or service they're about to receive is top-notch. But your manager expects you to instill confidence in the company and its products at all times to customers. What will you say to the next caller?

Or how would you handle it if the staff you support asked you to fill in the odometer readings on travel expense reports – not with real readings they give you, but with estimates you base on travel distance and contrived odometer figures? Is this okay, especially when this will be a signed legal document with the traveler's signature at the bottom attesting to its accuracy and truthfulness? After all, it's not you signing it.

Or what about the personal assistant left with the inference from her manager that she should be evasive on the phone with the manager's spouse about where she is at or who she is with. This is because the manager is blurring business and personal issues at work. If you were that assistant, how far would you go in saying your manager is not available and cannot be reached?

Or what if you are offered a gift by a coworker or client? Should you consider why, such as if there is a motive behind the gift beyond typical thoughtfulness? Can you accept it (per your company's guidelines too), and if not will you return it?

Some of those examples may not be clear ethical issues. Only you can decide what is and isn't an ethical issue for you in some cases. Clearly if someone asks you to give her money out of the cash register of the business you both work for so she can buy lunch for herself and friends (and it's not the owner), you're facing an ethical situation and an illegal one. Your response is going to be an easy, "No, get lost." Unfortunately, all ethical situations aren't that clear. Expect to face gray ethical situations as well as black and white ones.

Replies to Use in Situations That Affect Your Ethics

Sometimes resolving an ethical dilemma is as easy (or hard for some) as turning to a person and assertively saying, "That's not in my comfort zone to xyz. What is another way we can handle this?"

Or say, "Thank you but I can't accept this gift because xyz."

Those responses work with rational people. Not everyone is rational. Sometimes your ethics could cost you your job or a business relationship. Is that bad? Perhaps not when you consider that you have to live with your ethical-related choices and behavior for life whereas you can always get another job during your lifetime. Or you can always make other business relationship contacts during your lifetime, but you can't push replay on a poor ethical-related decision you made. That's done, once done.

Therefore, never let anyone push you into crossing ethical lines with moral or legal implications that will affect you or others aversely. Know your ethical boundaries; communicate about them to others when necessary. If your gut is telling you something is uncomfortable about a particular situation, listen to your gut. Explore that discomfort in your gut to find the best direction for you to go in. Take a short time-out if needed to think before you act or react to a request or situation.

You Won't Cross Boundaries

Boundaries are limits. They constitute what's acceptable to you and what is not acceptable, even deal-breakers. The last section discussed giving thought to ethical boundaries. You have more boundaries too in personal and professional life that aren't necessarily related to ethical matters. For instance, boundaries could be related to separating your work life from your home life in order to provide you with work and personal life balance.

It's important to develop boundaries in the workplace because not doing so can lead to job dissatisfaction, stress, even job burnout. Therefore, knowing and enforcing your personal and professional boundaries increases your job satisfaction. The right boundaries can even increase your productivity on the job through more effective time usage.

You also set boundaries to create work/life balance in order to maintain your mental and physical health as well as a level of personal privacy in the workplace. Without good health, you're not an effective worker (and your personal life suffers too).

Setting and Maintaining Boundaries as an Admin

There are many boundaries you'll want to develop and set in your administrative role to get the benefits (and avoid the downfalls) noted above. The need to have, communicate, and enforce boundaries arises on a regular occasion in the workplace. You don't "set them and forget them." While some boundaries are best set early in a job or with those new to your support, you also can set and develop boundaries ongoing in your work life. The following are some example scenarios of when you'll want to have clearly defined boundaries in your mind (that you then enforce), including some situations administrative professionals often encounter:

SCENARIO: Managers and coworkers you support call you at home — and at all hours.

BOUNDARIES: Will you take calls on weekends? How late on week days? How will you communicate this to those you support?

SCENARIO: Your teenager or a friend calls you at work multiple times a day, interfering with your productivity and getting you concerned looks from your manager.

BOUNDARIES: If you keep taking all of her calls, you are not enforcing any boundaries, and the ultimate effect is lower workplace productivity for you. In order to reverse this negative effect, you have to communicate that you're not available 24/7 with the exception of emergencies.

SCENARIO: You check your workplace e-mail at home and respond to it after hours.

BOUNDARIES: You've just created the expectations from managers and coworkers that you'll keep doing this, even if it's not timely or an emergency. Is this the message you were trying to communicate?

SCENARIO: A coworker comments that because you're administrative staff, you don't have any real impact on the big picture results of the company.

BOUNDARIES: How will your respond? You teach people how to treat you. Therefore you say, "Ok, I agree," if you don't speak up based on your boundaries for tolerating disrespect — or simply misconceptions by others.

SCENARIO: Your manager or coworker just invited you to connect on Facebook.

BOUNDARIES: How will you differentiate between "friends" and "friendliness" related to your workplace? How will you communicate no if that's your response?

SCENARIO: A manager or coworker asks you to do something personal for her on company time.

BOUNDARIES: Where do your job responsibilities begin and end? How do you convey this differentiation between work and favors, and on the clock and off?

SCENARIO: Your coworkers' break-time chatter turns into gossip about other employees or customers.

BOUNDARIES: Will you keep listening? Will you walk away? At what point?

Ultimately, you must know and be willing to communicate and enforce your boundaries in order for them to be effective. People will stretch your boundaries. That's how they learn the limits of what they can do around you or ask you to do for them. That's how they achieve respect for you too sometimes — by watching how you carry yourself in the workplace and how you communicate, including responding to breaches of your boundaries.

The way to enforce your boundaries is politely, tactfully, and assertively. Don't make others feel they have done something wrong if they overstep your boundaries. Watch your tone and choose your words with care. Handle each matter with grace and dignity so both you and the other person feel respected when and if you draw that line. Communicating boundaries is part of developing good working business relationships, even partnerships with those you support.

Saying No For All the Right Reasons

Administrative professionals can be people pleasers. You serve in your role. You want to please your customer. You like to and want to help people. Therefore, saying no isn't always in every administrative professional's vocabulary. But it should be for lots of good reasons. That includes some reasons talked about earlier such as to avoid taking on more work than you can handle or taking on assignments with conflicting deadlines. Saying yes to something you can't do like that neither helps you nor the other person. Plus the quality of the finished product is likely to suffer (if it ever gets finished).

Sometimes you also need to say no to assignments that are not within your ethical or personal or professional boundaries. You *can* do them, but you *won't* do them for those reasons, even when you like and respect the person asking for such assistance. Don't be afraid to say no because when you do so for all the right reasons and in the right manner, you are behaving assertively and coming from an authentic place of integrity. You are not pushing back against a manager for negative reasons nor being malicious to a coworker or customer. Oftentimes, you gain respect when saying no for the right reasons and in the right way.

Perhaps your assistant manager has asked you to make 25 copies of a one-page, two-sided program for her child's play. That's simple enough and doesn't use a lot of paper. But you won't do things like that because it's using the company's ink and it's using your time "on the clock" for a coworker's personal benefit. So you say no: "I prefer not to make personal copies on the company's machine and time." If you feel the need to soften your no, say "I prefer not to make personal copies on the company's machine and time without permission from [my manager]. You'll need to ask him if I can take time out to do that for you. If he says yes, of course, I'll be happy to help you out."

It could be something as simple as you don't want to go to lunch with a coworker who keeps asking you. While it can be good to mingle with coworkers at luncheons, sometimes you may have a personal reason you just don't want to mingle off-site with this person. You don't want to and you won't. Simply say no: "*No. Thanks for asking me but I have other plans for lunch.*" Be a polite, broken record every time you're asked. You don't need to say more than that. "So you can't go," your coworker adds. You say: "I have other plans, so no. Thanks for asking though."

A coworker asks you to "cover for her" by telling the boss she went to run an errand when really she left early. You can say, "No, I won't lie for you if [our manager] directly asks me."

A coworker wants you to do some of her work for her and says, "Can you help me out today and do this for me?" You don't have the time, and you know she does: "No, I wish I could help you out, but I've got a big to-do list of my own today." She says, "But I really need your help." You say: "Unfortunately, I've got a big load too. You should ask your manager if he can help you re-prioritize your workload today if it's too much due at the same time. He may be able to help you with that."

Your manager wants you to stay late to receive a delivery from the printer, but you have to pick up your child. You say, "No, I can't because I have to pick up my child." Your manager says you are the only one available to do it. You repeat, "No, I will not be able to stay late because I'm the only one available to pick up my child."

Sometimes you need to say no, regardless of consequences and pending your priorities. People in the workplace will push you to do things because they are trying to get their workplace needs met, not always considering your needs or wants. Say, "No, I won't do that," when you need to say it. If you can think of an alternative to help the person you're saying no to (and an alternative is appropriate), offer one: "No [manager name], I cannot stay late because I'm the only one available to pick up my child. I have an idea though. If you tell me which printer, I can call the printer now before I leave and ask the printer to hold the delivery for me to pick up on the way into work tomorrow morning."

Here's another example: Someone asks you to volunteer for a committee that does nothing for your career goals and it is not of personal interest. Unless you owe the person a favor, it's okay to say no: "Thank you for asking me but I decline." Got an alternative? Say: "Thank you for asking me but I decline. However, you might want to ask Suzy. I don't know her availability, but I do know she has some experience in that subject matter [or say whatever reason caused you to think of Suzy]."

Don't forget the "broken record" method if the person continues: "So you don't want to be on the committee?" You reply: "No, I don't want to be on the committee, but thanks for asking me."

If you need to communicate you won't do something or just don't want to do something, then you need to be able to communicate the word no, or at least communicate other words and phrases that clearly mean no. And you need to be able to say it assertively (i.e. not aggressively or passively). It's your right to say no. Just say it!

Say it in the same neutral tone as you would any other conversation. Don't make saying no seem like an issue. Saying no is part of ordinary conversation unless for some reason you put emphasis on the "no," making it seem otherwise. Don't do that. Just calmly and politely say no and move onward in your conversation. With practice it'll become just another word you use as appropriate when responding to people. After all, it takes as much effort (or as little effort) to say no as yes and vice versa.

***

Chapter 7 Recap:

- Administrative professionals serve and thus are often nurturing in nature. Take care not to lose yourself in serving others.
- Define your ethics, and decline to do anything unethical.
- Maintain professional boundaries in the workplace and teach others, perhaps gently if possible, not to cross your personal and professional boundaries.
- Learn to say no to what you won't do.
- No is not a positive word, but it's not a bad word.
- Recognize that two people can have different value systems and can still work side by side. Yet you still need to set and enforce your professional ethical boundaries.
- Your ethical standards and issues in the workplace can rank minor to major, and you don't have to turn every one of them into a "stand your ground" ethics situation. Thoughtfully decide when you must take action to announce or enforce your ethical boundary.
- All ethical situations aren't black and white clear; some are gray.
- Sometimes standing up for your ethical boundaries can cost you a job or business relationship. That's not necessarily a bad thing. Those things come and go; your memories of your ethical decisions are with you for life.
- You will need to set and maintain other personal and professional boundaries too (in addition to ethical ones). You need to communicate these boundaries ongoing in your work life.

- Managers and coworkers learn the limits of what they can do around you or ask you to do for them by the boundaries you set and enforce (and vice-versa).
- Don't make others feel they have done something wrong if they do overstep your boundaries. Correct and enforce boundaries politely, tactfully, and assertively.
- Saying no should be in an administrative professional's vocabulary for lots of reasons. The reasons go beyond just saying no to assignments that are not within your ethical or personal or professional boundaries. For instance, you may have to say no in regard to an unreasonable work deadline or to a coworker's offer of lunch together.
- Oftentimes, you gain respect when saying no for the right reasons and in the right way.
- It's your right to say no assertively.

Chapter 8

Communicating What You Can't and Won't Say

Just like with saying, no, you won't do something, you need to be able to say, no, you can't do or say something. When you're an assistant – and the higher the level, the more this applies – lots of people want to know what you know. However, they don't always *need* to know what you know (they just *want* to know). Sometimes they don't have the right to know the information because it's confidential between you and someone else (i.e. your executive, your company, a coworker). Also, on occasion you simply have to communicate you can't say something because you don't know the answer. Below is more on this topic and some communication strategies you can use to say, "I can't tell, won't tell, or don't know."

Maintaining Confidences

Assistants – particularly executive assistants – know a lot of information about what their executives are working on or with whom they are working; sometimes this is confidential information, at least until your executive is ready to go public with it. In addition, all types of assistants encounter privileged information that the company may not want released to everyone or anyone just yet. Some assistants who have close working relationships with their executives even know personal information about their executives that should remain private.

However, people inside of your company and outside of your company will still ask you for any or all of these types of information. They are free to do so. It's how you reply that matters. Below are some responses administrative professionals can use to indicate they will not answer the question. Tweak them and make them your own words to use as needed.

- I'm not at liberty to say.
- I can't share that information with you because that would be breaking my promise to someone else that I'd keep it confidential.
- I cannot deny or confirm information on that topic because it's not within my authority to do so.
- That's a topic I don't have authority to discuss freely.
- The information is not mine to share, so let's discuss something else.
- I can't tell you that. If I told you about someone else's private matters, then you would be right not to trust me in the future with confidential matters you tell me.
- I can't give out that information, but I can pass along your request for it to [executive name here].

While that last response is perfectly acceptable for people interested in legitimately getting the information, it's also a deterrent to those who don't need the information. In that case, they will probably tell you to not bother, they can make do without it. Request closed!

Responding to "Tricks"

Sometimes people probe deliberately for information from assistants in sneaky ways like these:

Reciprocity — This is when a coworker shares personal information with you purposely intending to get you to reciprocate with a similar story. For example, she says: "My boss is so demanding. Yesterday he asked me for three project updates and he only gave me all three projects two hours earlier. He exhausts me sometimes." Your natural instinct may be to say: "I know what you mean. Yesterday my boss asked me...." Don't!

Your Reply: Instead, just close the topic with an empathetic or positive remark, and change the conversation topic to something more neutral (if you plan to continue conversing with the person): "Oh well, you'll work it out. By the way, do you know how to do xyz? I tried to do it yesterday but couldn't get it quite right."

Awkward Silence — In this instance, you briefly answer a question or reply to a comment from someone. Then that person stays silent or repeats the response and says, "Hmmm...I see." The object of this tactic is that you will feel the need to fill the awkward silence, the void in the conversation, and start babbling information, even sharing information you shouldn't. It can be very revealing for the first party since you are answering questions he or she didn't even know to ask.

Your Reply: Stay quiet but attentive with your body language and facial expressions. Don't fill the void. Or consider asking a transitional, specific question such as, "Is there anything else you'd like to know on the topic?" Or "Is there anything else I can help you with?"

Incorrect Information — This scenario is when someone intentionally says something incorrect to you in hopes you'll instinctively respond back with the correct information. For example, a coworker says, "Is your manager back from Phoenix yet?" He knows your manager is not in Phoenix; he wants to know where your manager is or what he's doing because of rumors of pending company reorganization or mergers. He wants you to say: "Jay isn't in Phoenix. He went to Boston for a meeting at headquarters." And the back and forth conversation continues from there. A person does this when he knows you probably wouldn't reveal the information if asked outright for it.

Your Reply: One way to have prevented this leakage (if it was confidential information) might have been to reply to the question like this: "No, Jay didn't go to Phoenix. Do you need to speak with him about something right away? If so, I can put you on his calendar for a conference call." Or say even less: "No, Jay isn't back in the office. Can I help you in his place with something?"

Many people may be sincere when they speak in any of these three ways; others may be probing for confidential information. Be aware so you respond with deliberate thought and not instinctive replies.

Answering Questions You Can't Actually Answer

It often seems administrative professionals know a little bit about everything in the office. Therefore, you're the "go to" person when coworkers and managers have questions about how to do something or where to locate something. When customers call, you often take the call and respond to their questions or direct them to someone who can do so. It's the same for when vendors call. You are everyone's go-to person, as is often the case for many administrative professionals. This frontline role commands that scenario.

Because this is the case in your administrative role, you've heard many of the same inquiries and questions multiple times. Perhaps you've heard them to the point where you really don't even need to wait for someone to finish her question to you (but you politely wait anyway). However, every once in a while, someone asks you something you don't know. Pleasant challenge or not, you have to communicate that you don't know. Here are some suggestions for responding:

- I don't know the answer to your question. Let me ask my manager and get back to you by the end of the day.
- That's a good question and one I don't know the answer to. Let me research it to find out the answer and call you back by the end of the day.
- That is something I don't know, but I know someone who does know. I'll call you back within the hour with what I can find out from my contact.

- That is something I don't know, but I know someone who does know. I can give you that person's name and contact information if you'd like it.

- I don't know how that's done here. Let me get one of my coworkers to explain the process to me so I can explain it to you. I'm sure others will be asking me that too in the future.

- I think I know the answer to your question but I don't want to give you wrong information. I'll get back to you in an hour after I confirm what I think I know.

- I've never encountered that and don't know how it's done. Do you want me to find out?

- This process is new to me. I'll ask [name] to show me so I can start handling this for you and answering your questions about it.

- I don't know what to tell people who call and ask me [fill in the blank]. What do you suggest? Is there a standard response the company uses?

Note that several of the responses suggested above are variations of the popular response, "I don't know, but I'll find out." The difference is you're adding a timeline. People want to know when you'll find out and when you'll get back to them. Offer the timeline; don't make them ask. Then get back in touch with the person (whether face to face, phone or e-mail) by your deadline even if it's to tell that person you're still researching the answer. Give that person the status update to her inquiry if you promised to try to find an answer.

"That person" may be a coworker, manager, executive, client/customer, or vendor. As the administrative professional, you interact with all of those people, and often they think you know all the answers. Give them an answer, even if it's one of the "I don't know" responses listed above. Don't fake it, or guess if you don't know the answer. In that case, you will be remembered for giving out incorrect information long after you would have been forgotten for not knowing the answer. Communicate strategically to help people even when you can't help them much and to maintain your personal brand in your administrative career.

***

Chapter 8 Recap:

- Sometimes as an assistant you need to be able to say no because you can't do or say something. Sometimes you need to say you simply don't know the answer.

- All assistants, especially executive assistants, are privy to confidential information, even personal information about those they support.

- People inside or outside of your company are free to ask you for confidential or private information; that doesn't mean you need to answer them. It's how you reply that matters.

- There is more than one way to say, "I'm not at liberty to say." Try out a variety of phrases and find ones that work for you and your situations.

- Beware of people who deliberately probe for information from assistants in sneaky ways so you don't fall for communication tactics that thrive on your instinctive replies. Respond to all inquiries with deliberate thought.

- Administrative professionals are rightfully seen as the "go-to" persons in the office by just about everyone because they know a little about everything and are on the frontline. It's probably the same in your case. However, that doesn't mean you actually do know about everything. But you can find out. Learn the different ways to say so.

- When you say you don't know and will find out, offer a specific timeline and be there when that time is up with a status update on the inquiry.

Chapter 9

Communicating What You Need
On The Job

There are a lot of things you need as an administrative professional to perform your work to the satisfaction of those you support as well as to your own satisfaction. Most of these needs involve communicating successfully with other people. "Successfully" means getting the results you intended: your needs met. With an assertive demeanor and the right communication strategy, you can get what you need. Try these communication scenarios and strategies if they fit your needs:

Adherence to Your Deadlines

It's frustrating when you're trying to lead without explicit or positional authority sometimes. One instance is when you need documents, information and input from others in the company (or elsewhere) by certain dates in order to accomplish your assignments or portions of projects. However, sometimes those people seem to ignore your deadlines. So what can you do to "enforce" your deadlines? Here are two tactics:

Set Clear Deadlines

When writing, or verbally expressing deadlines, be specific. Don't use "today," "tomorrow," or "ASAP (as soon as possible)." Instead, use actual dates and times, especially in written correspondence. Readers may be in different time zones than you or read your e-mail on a day you didn't write it. This misunderstanding could result in non-adherence to your deadlines.

Also, be specific when confirming travel reservations with all parties involved. In that case, use the day of the week too (it'll help catch errors, maybe even your own too).

Relay Consequences to Encourage Action

You can use this tactic in writing a document or speaking with someone. It may encourage the other party to meet your deadline or other needs you name. You can structure your sentence with phrasing that has positive consequences or negative consequences:

Positive consequences: If I receive your completed travel expense statement by 5 p.m. Tuesday, then I can have your reimbursement check to you by Friday.

Negative consequences: If I do not receive your completed travel expense statement by 5 p.m. Tuesday, then I cannot process it in time for you to receive your funds reimbursed by Friday.

Note that the statements above are neutral "I" statements and not accusatory "you" statements (i.e. If *you* don't do this, then *you* will cause that to happen). A person may miss your message (and deadline) if she is reacting with anger because you are seemingly accusing her of something with "you" statements. Communicate strategically to get the results you need using "I" statements, specific wording for deadlines, and stated consequences.

Setting Priorities With Your Manager

You are already doing several timely assignments for your manager or executive when he brings one more by your desk for you to do. Now is the time to speak up. If you're doing another priority task, then say: "I will need to stop working on the ABC project you gave me in order to get this new assignment done by lunch. Is that okay with you?"

Your manager may have forgotten about the first task or think you already finished it. He may not want you to quit working on the first project, or he may give one of the tasks to someone else.

Clarification of an Assignment

The key here is that *you* need to be clear when asking for clarity from others. The best way to do that is by using specific language. Here's an example of being nonspecific vs. specific with your words and phrases:

Nonspecific: I don't understand what you mean by this assignment request. Can you explain it?

Specific: I read the instructions you sent me by e-mail to do assignment X. Now I need to clarify a few related items to make sure the outcome meets your expectations. When you wrote X, did you mean you wanted me to also get Jerry's direct input on this issue or just if I needed his assistance? Also, you said Y, and I remembered last year when we did the Z project, you liked X. Do you want me to try to work X into the results too?

If you write that specific conversation in e-mail, format it so it's not all one paragraph. Number the questions and put each as its own paragraph. If you speak that specific conversation to your manager, pause between questions. Let your manager answer the first question before you toss out the second one to him. Spacing and pausing add clarity when you have several things to ask at once, even on the same topic as in that scenario.

Asking Your Busy Boss Many Questions

"Bundle" your questions and updates. That means prepare to ask your manager or executive several questions – even if unrelated topics – in one sitting (or likely "standing" with a busy boss). Don't interrupt your manager with each question separately throughout the day. Most executives hate that!

Organize your questions on a page under subtopics. Agree on a standing meeting time, such as twice a day, for delivering and discussing them at once. If your manager has a different work style and work hours, he may appreciate you sending the list of questions by e-mail. If you don't have a regularly scheduled meeting but need to ask a bunch of unrelated questions now and then, still bundle them and ask them at one time during the day.

Important: Put the subtopics in order of priority in case your manager or executive doesn't get through all of them during your meeting or when reading your e-mail.

Getting Buy-in to Change a Process

You know a more efficient way to do a procedure that's always been done a certain way in your office (even since before you arrived as the newest office administrator). But your manager or coworkers balk at the idea of "change" and suggest you "don't go there." So what do you do to get buy-in for your forward thinking?

You stop calling it "change," which is a concept many people find scary. Many people don't want to "change." So instead of using the word "change," simply call it "an experiment." For instance, say: "I have a little experiment I want to try with your help to see if it works for our staff when doing xyz...."

That communication strategy may sound simple, even a little silly, but you'll be surprised at how changing one word or a phrase can change how someone receives or hears a message.

Better Communication With Your Manager

In order to develop better communication with your manager or executive, you have to purposely and regularly communicate. It really is that simple. It needs to be meaningful communication that has specific purpose. You can't work as a team (i.e. you and your executive) if both of you don't communicate much or ever. That's just separate individuals existing in the same space working on separate tasks independently.

Ask for a daily huddle or official meeting – however you want to phrase it. But the bottom line is that you need to get this on the calendar and make it a priority.

Tell your executive: "I want to keep you in the loop with status updates you need to know. Likewise, I want to make sure I know all that's going on with your workday and goals so I can best support you as your assistant. I think we can do this best with a short meeting every morning for perhaps about 15 minutes. Are you agreeable to that?"

If your manager or executive is at a remote location, meet by video conference or telephone in the morning. The reason mornings are the best time to meet is because neither you nor your executive really knows with certainty how the rest of the day will flow. You may not get to this meeting later in the day.

If you can't get together in the afternoon for a second huddle, send a status update by e-mail. Make it a compilation of all that your manager or executive needs to know at the end of the day, including any calendar reminders for the next morning if necessary. Whether meeting in person or sending e-mail compilations, always discuss or write the priority items first. This is because you or your executive could get interrupted and not get to the end of your discussion list.

Communicate With a "Get to the Point" Work Style

Many executives are often "get to the point" work styles, and other people you interact with may be too. When dealing with someone who skims correspondence or who talks and/or writes in short, hurried sound bites, just give her the facts quickly and concisely. Start with the point (verbally or in writing). Don't lead into it; just "go." Tell your manager the main thing you need her to know and make that the first thing you tell her. Then expand on your message as needed or time allows.

If you're writing e-mail, put that main message concisely in the subject line as well as in the first sentence of the e-mail. If you need the reader or listener to take action, start with that action needed. Use bullet points in written material. If you have a lot to write about, start with a brief executive summary; even one sentence is fine but it could be one or two short paragraphs.

Be in The Loop

You need to attend department meetings to stay in the loop on projects and deadlines. You know that! But does your manager or executive know that? Tell him: "Typically, I'm going to be helping you get your next project 'out the door.' So I need to continuously know what projects you're working on and the issues, due dates and status, and what's coming up. That way I can more efficiently manage my priorities and make sure my schedule is clear to start helping. Rather than you always having to take your time to fill me in, I can get some of this information firsthand by attending your staff meetings or project meetings as deemed appropriate by you."

You might want to add this too: "Also, if you share your notes or minutes from meetings I can't attend, then I can stay in the loop that way too. It's like this: The more I know what's going on with your projects and what you've assigned your team, the better I can assist you and without you having to stop to explain things to me."

Asking Your Multiple Managers to Get in Synch

If you're being stretched and stressed too frequently, call a group huddle composed of you and all of your managers or executives at once. Some administrative professionals have chosen to host a meeting of their managers when workloads got too muddled. Those administrative professionals say it was a successful strategy – but also that it's a tactic to use sparingly.

Try to work out your workload and scheduling and prioritization on your own first. Then if you do call a meeting, bring potential solutions to it. Explain to your managers or executives what's happening. Get their recommendations because it's the nature of managers and executives to offer their input and you should listen to it. If they like your solutions and tweak them a bit, run with their changes – as long as all the executives are in agreement. Your goal is to get them all in synch with what's going on in terms of utilizing your talents and time.

If you need a visual to show existing workloads in black and white (e.g. percentages, duties), prepare a chart before the meeting to hand out. This will get the group huddle off to an organized start.

Here is example phrasing you can use for your mini presentation/huddle: "I called this huddle today to discuss my workload and your needs in relation to my assistance. I want your input. Here is a chart that shows my current status of 'supply vs. demand' for my assistance. As you can see, demand is exceeding supply these days. I'm hoping we can fix that in this meeting and all become in synch with what I'm doing and what I'm needed to be doing. I'll give you my thoughts on a potential solution. I also want your input. Shall I go first or does anyone want to precede me with their thoughts?"

Manage Conflicting Priorities from Multiple Managers

In some instances, it may be wise as the administrative professional to simply stay out of the middle of management. That means step aside and have managers and executives discuss conflicting deadlines or priorities among themselves without you present. Just directly tell the last person giving you something to do with urgency the truth about your prioritization of projects for the day and workload. Use facts and tactful phrasing, but essentially pass the dilemma back into that manager's or executive's corner for a decision.

For instance, say: "Jay, I can start work on your slide presentation later today, but right now it's not possible for me to get a first draft of it to you by early this afternoon. The reason is [executive] Bob asked me to do some research and preparation for a meeting he's leading this week, and it's already almost noon. Why don't you talk to Bob, and see if he's flexible with me setting aside his work for a couple of hours to help you now. Whatever you two decide is fine with me."

Get Your Ideas Heard and Taken Seriously

Many employees — administrative professionals included — get upset or frustrated when they believe they're relaying important information or a good idea to their managers or others and yet their ideas aren't implemented. Often when speaking up with such an idea, you may believe you're being ignored too. Perhaps you blame this on your position. For instance, you think, "If I were a department manager and not a department administrative assistant, then he'd listen and give me more respect." But is that the case always? Is that what's going on in every such situation?

For instance, you have a great idea for saving money on the company phone bill. You're eager to tell your executive. So the next time he stops by your desk, you plan to quickly blurt out your idea while you have his attention.

Bad idea!

Your executive isn't coming to your desk to hear your idea because he doesn't know you have one. Don't interrupt his haste and train of thought with your need. Also because you recognize that your executive is busy, you may speak quickly and ramble in an attempt to get your idea quickly out there. That will impede clarity of your idea and thus your executive's perception of it. Your idea may be ignored in this scenario because you delivered a bad presentation at a bad time, not because of anything related to your administrative position and hierarchy in the company.

How you present your idea — and also when and where — can affect the reception of you and your idea. If you have a great idea but present it poorly and/or at the wrong time and place, that could be a deciding factor in if you get heard or if your idea gets credence.

Try this: Draft your idea into a one-page proposal. Include terminology your executive understands. Include points that would be of most interest to your executive. Then approach your executive and ask to meet with him for 10 minutes about an idea you have for [fill in the blank.] Leave the one-page handout with your executive if he requests it in writing or if you want him to have a recap to review on his time again later.

Present one idea at a time and not multiple ideas in one session, especially if they're on unrelated topics. Keep it simple. Make your idea come from you, and express it with confidence. Don't say, "I don't know if this is something you'd want to do." Instead say, "Here's what I'd like to do," or "Here's how I thought we could handle this."

Tell your manager what's needed to implement your idea, how you'll do it and what support you need from him. End your presentation with an open-ended question, such as, "So what do you think?" Don't end with a leading and closed question such as, "Do you like the idea?"

Finally, be open to collaborating further on the idea.

Know How to Deliver Negative Feedback

You may be a lead admin supervising a team of administrative professionals, you may be leading a group of volunteers, or you may be a special project leader. These are all positions in which you as an administrative professional may have to deliver feedback, both positive and negative feedback. You may even just find yourself in some situation as a coworker in which you believe you need to give another coworker, perhaps even a manager, some feedback that's not so positive. All of these scenarios can be tough.

If you've ever received negative feedback, you know it can be hard to hear at times, especially if you're not used to hearing it. Even seasoned administrative professionals have a hard time hearing negative feedback. Many of us are sensitive persons despite trying to be objective professionals on the clock. After all, we are the same person on and off the clock.

Likewise, it's equally hard for many of us to deliver negative feedback. Praise is so much easier to give than negative feedback or constructive criticism, and even saying nothing at all is easier at times. But easy isn't always best. If you find yourself on the verge of giving negative feedback, try these tips:

Target the behavior, not the person.

It's about what's happening and the results of the behavior, actions, event, task, etc. It's not about personalities (i.e. "You always act this way"; or "You never let me...").

Don't criticize what can't be changed.

What's done is done. If you can't think of a specific way your feedback will help in the future, don't offer it. Negative feedback is only useful if somehow the behavior, event, etc., will be repeated in the future and you can help change the outcome with your feedback.

Couch your feedback in gentle sentence structure.

For example say: "You might consider doing 'this' at the next orientation session. That way...."

Consider the "sandwich method."

That's when you say something positive, followed by the negative feedback, and then followed by positive feedback. This can work for sensitive recipients who don't appreciate or can't handle blunt directness. However, only use this method when you have sincere positive feedback to give.

You Need [fill in the blank]

Whatever it is you need to get your job done and to meet the expectations of your manager or executive, you need to ask for it. If your need is work-related and will benefit the quality of the results you will be presenting, it's perfectly acceptable for you to communicate your need to your manager or executive. In fact, if your manager or executive knew you had such a need, he'd be expecting you to speak up and tell him. Neither administrative professionals nor their managers and executives are mind-readers.

***

Chapter 9 Recap:
- To get what you need on the job to do your job, you will need to communicate successfully with other people. *Successfully* means you get the result you need.
- When you need adherence to deadlines, write or say due dates as specifically as possible and relay positive or negative consequences of meeting, or not meeting, those deadlines.

- Communicate priorities – or re-communicate them ongoing – because your manager may keep giving you assignments without remembering specifically what he already asked you to do. Reprioritization is needed ongoing sometimes.

- When asking for clarity on assignments or anything, be specific with your questions. Don't speak with non-specific, general phrasing such as "Can you explain this further?"

- Learn how to bundle your questions and updates for busy bosses and to prioritize the list or agenda. Most important goes first – in case time runs out.

- Realize how changing one word or phrase can put people at ease, lower their defensive instincts, and get cooperation. For instance, use the phrase "Let's try an experiment" instead of "We need to change" or "You need to change."

- Purposely and regularly communicate with your manager or executive. Otherwise, you're just separate individuals existing in the same space working on separate tasks independently and not a team or business partners.

- If your executive wants information to the point, give her the facts quickly and concisely and start with the point or bottom line. Just go! This is for verbal or written communication.

- If you're not "in the loop" in your office and in your executive and administrative professional business relationship, get in it. Explain to your manager why you need to be in that loop and how this can be done.

- Call a group huddle of your multiple managers if you need to get them in synch with supply versus demand of you.

- If you have two managers vying for the same deadline by you, then ask the last one giving you something to work it out directly with the other manager and get back to you with any reprioritization approval. Stay out of the middle!

- In order that your ideas are properly heard and given credence by your manager or executive, you must present them at appropriate times and locations. Also present just one idea, one topic, at a time.

- Even administrative professionals deliver negative feedback because sometimes it's necessary to do so. When you do, target the behavior and not the person. Plus only give negative feedback if somehow the behavior or event will be repeated. Otherwise, what's done is done; move on.

- Whatever it is you need to get your job done and to meet the expectations of your manager or executive, you need to ask for it. You need to! Nobody reads minds in the office.

Chapter 10

Communicating What You Want In Your Career

I t's okay to ask for things you *want* in your administrative career. Key words there are "your career." You must define your own career and your wants related to it. Don't let others define your career for you or wait around to see what happens in your career. Work your career management on your timeline, not someone else's timeline. Go after what you want when you want it.

Ask others to help you get what you want when it's appropriate and they can willingly play a role. The worst case scenario: You won't get what you want or someone will say no. That's not a problem, really. That's life. It has challenges and twists and turns. Just alter your objectives to meet your same goals and keep striving to get what you want. There is more than one route to career fulfillment. Plus, new routes open up all the time.

Keep looking forward, not backward. You may not be feeling much satisfaction from 25 "No's" you received so far from your efforts; however, that one "Yes" you will get eventually is sure going to feel good when it happens.

So what do you want in your role and career? What do other administrative professionals want in their careers? Maybe it's the same thing, speaking big picture; your specifics may be different. A lot of administrative professionals say they want more (or any) opportunities for professional development, an increase in salary or wages, and a defined administrative (or other) career path in the company or administrative field. Do you want any of those things too? If so, try these communication strategies to ask for what you want or for help in getting what you want:

Funding to Attend a Conference

You want to attend an administrative professional development or training conference, seminar or workshop. You want to do so on company time (but if it's a good one and runs into your weekend, that's fine too). You want your company to pay for it. Is that too much to ask?

Not at all, assuming there is some ROI (return on investment) for your employer and you can state it ahead of time and demonstrate it upon return. Will the answer be "yes"? Maybe or maybe not. But it'll definitely be "no" if you don't ask (an unstated "no" because nobody knows there even is a conference or that you want to go and why).

So how do you ask your manager to let you attend this conference and have the company pay for it? Try this communication strategy:

Be assertive; be direct. Don't ask, "Would you mind if I attended this administrative professional conference in June?"

That's meek and passive. That's also not giving a reason you should attend the conference.

Don't ask, "What do you think about me attending this administrative professional conference?"

You already know you want to attend the conference. You're not really asking *what do you think* as in give me an opinion.

When asking to attend and for payment of administrative professional development and training conferences, seminars and workshops, you must speak with confidence and clarity. Plus with busy executives and managers, you must be to the point. Ask the questions that will get you the answers you need. The above questions do not do that.

Instead say: "There is an administrative professional conference in June I'd like to attend. Some of the session topics are a, b and c. What I learn at those sessions could really help me support you better in regard to learning better ways to manage your calendar and scheduling, and/or fill in the blank here. Would you approve me attending on company time, and will the company pay for it?"

Now shut up and wait for your manager to respond. Don't devalue what you just said or add confusion to your neatly conveyed request by rambling on to fill any silence. Let your manager think. Let him respond. Make sure you have done all your background research on your request so that you will be able to answer any question on the topic from your manager. Make those answers succinct.

Face-to-face communication is always best for these scenarios. You can answer questions on the spot and rebut any concerns. You can read body language and gestures. You're more likely to get an immediate response. However, if you must or want to e-mail your request, that's okay too. If you have trouble speaking clearly without a case of nerves, you can e-mail your request – and that may be best for you. E-mail is still communication and perhaps it's an even better communication strategy if you and your manager or executive best operate that way or remotely. Do what's best in your situation. Only you know that.

A Raise in Your Salary or Wages

Most administrative professionals welcome an increase in salary but fewer actually ask for a raise. Therefore they don't get one, or they get a tiny routine salary increase given to all staff annually. It can feel intimidating asking someone else to give you more of their money (i.e. the company's money). That's why you need a communication strategy for this conversation versus just winging it.

Before you can devise the actual words you'll use to ask for an increase in salary, you have to do the background research. Essentially, you're giving a presentation (albeit a mini one) and as with all presentations you create, you need the background information to go into it. You'll also want to anticipate the Q&A session that usually follows a presentation. In the case of asking for a raise, that may turn into a negotiation session. Or it may be a request for clarification or more information on your points in your presentation.

So for the background research, you need to decide how much of a salary increase you're aiming for specifically and how you will justify that salary or wage. For how much, decide on a monetary range you'd be satisfied with and start by suggesting the high end (you also could state it in terms of a percentage increase). If you get that figure, then that's fantastic. More likely, your employer will negotiate downward if he agrees to a raise at all. That's why you start a little higher than perhaps you think is justified or that you can get. Also, don't just ask for a raise in general; ask for a specific figure. And be flexible.

The justification for the increase in salary should be totally based on your merits: your accomplishments and responsibilities. Sometimes it's useful to include general salary or wage figures in your field, industry and geographical area for positions with comparable skills to yours (e.g. administrative, hospital, Northeast USA). That's if your current salary is lower than those figures you find during research. Some salary Web sites where you might find this type of information are listed in Appendix G.

It's the unique scenario and *rare* occasion in which you may want to mention the salary range of specific administrative personnel around you in the company. And that's only if it's freely available knowledge and your manager or executive is truly not aware that you're making less than the two assistants of the same stature, same tenure in the next office. Typically, this is not a recommended way to present yourself or your desire for a raise and won't reflect on you or your request favorably.

However, it would be unfair to you for me to say across the board that this scenario doesn't work ever. The reason is because I have seen instances in which including this information in a conversation with one's manager or executive did help promote the desired result. The clause though is that it is usually in a situation in which the administrative professional has a good partnership with her executive, and that executive is not the same boss of the other administrative professionals of similar stature.

However, if your boss is the manager over all three of you (or however many administrative professionals), he knows the individual salaries. In that case, it's best not to bring up this information with your manager or executive; if he wanted to make all three of you even, he would have voluntarily done that by now.

In general though, it is almost never a good idea to ask for money because Jill down the hall makes more money than you. The justification for your salary increase request should pertain to you, not what Jill makes nor what tasks she does in her administrative role. This conversation is about you. Keep the focus on you. Don't dilute the focus on you by speaking about other people in your company.

However, if you can find salary ranges for specific positions (not people) in your company, that is useful information you can use in your presentation. If you work in a large company or maybe a government organization, there is nothing preventing you from asking the human resources office about salary ranges for positions. Tell the HR staff person that you are requesting the information because you are managing your career; so you want to know the potential salary and positions for the various administrative levels in your company. Some HR office staff may answer this question. Some may not. If you don't ask, you won't know. Be candid and polite with your request.

In regard to further justifying your request for a salary increase based on your own merits, you need to think about how your duties and responsibilities have increased for the timeframe you've been at your current salary. About 20% increase in workload and responsibilities could be considered worthy of a raise. If you have accomplishments, especially outstanding ones in your opinion, this could be rationale for a raise. Maybe you can put into perspective what you've done to maximize your executive's time and enable him and the company to produce more. That could be raise-worthy.

If you are doing things that are of higher responsibility and decision-making levels, that could be worth a raise. If you've been meeting or exceeding mutually agreed-upon workplace goals, that could be raise request material. If you've recently increased your education (college degree, administrative certification, project management certification, software certification) and it benefits the company, talk about it. Your company may reward you or bring you up to the equivalent salary level of others with your educational background and current responsibilities.

Basically, if you want an outstanding raise, you need to be an outstanding employee. Mentally reverse your role and your manager's role, and look at you from that perspective too. If you were the manager or executive, would you give you a raise and why?

Also, when having a salary discussion, it's best to try to do it face to face with your manager. Schedule a meeting to discuss your salary and career aspirations (keep those aspirations within the current company for this talk).

Bring a one-page proposal to leave with your manager that makes your request courteously and documents your reasoning or argument support statements (e.g. 20% increase in workload, five new responsibilities listed, and perhaps noting any more advanced level work than before). Your manager may need to get approval from someone else, and this document will help him portray your conversation and merits accurately with his superior. Don't let your manager rely on his memory alone of your conversation. You know how busy he is and/or you know his memory; leave the facts with him in writing.

If you do not get a raise, still say "Thank you for your consideration." Don't complain. Skip saying, "Why not?" That two-word phrase probably won't get you the real information you need anyway. Instead, plan for getting a raise next request by directly asking this time, "What would I need to do to warrant a higher salary?" You can't work toward what you don't know about. Additionally, you may not want to keep chasing something not possible at your current company if that turns out to be the case. Ask. Listen. Communicate.

By planning and initiating conversations like these, you are actively managing your career on your schedule. It is key though that you use the right words and phrases (as well as timing and location) in your communication strategies. A few words different could get you a whole different response and thus results you don't want. Choose your phrasing strategically to get the exact information you're seeking.

Knowledge About Career Paths in the Company

You are an administrative professional and you want to remain an administrative professional. Or perhaps you want to move beyond the role to another position in the company. However, you don't know how to get there from where you're at. Or you don't know where "there" is.

What you need to do first is consult someone who should be an ally in your career aspirations: your boss. Having your manager or executive on your side can be very helpful and provide you with an indirect mentor for getting on a career path.

Certainly some managers don't want to see you go if you're good at what you do for them. That's a natural reaction. But those who understand career management, especially if they do it themselves, will be happy (maybe not ecstatic) to give you some input on your request. It's a career, not a marriage (although perhaps the executives who refer to their assistants as "job wives" or "second wives" don't get that).

Another reason you want your manager or executive as your ally in your career aspirations within the company is because he can be influential in recommending you. Of course your next prospective internal boss will talk to your current manager or executive. He may do so perhaps not just to find out what you can do but also to find out if "taking you away" would be detrimental to their business relationship. Office politics happen.

Schedule a face-to-face meeting with your manager to discuss career paths in the company and your career aspirations. This may be the first time your manager learns you have any. Like his assistant, he's not a mind-reader.

Your manager may have input about positions you are considering or even know of upcoming positions not yet listed publicly. Find out what the positions entail so you know if you'd like the work. These could even be in the department you're already working within. Together discuss the attributes and skills needed for these positions. Ask your manager if he would consider those attributes or skills to be your current strengths or weaknesses. Ask for objective views on your ability to learn what's needed for the next position up or lateral.

Be direct. Be open to feedback, not defensive. Choose your words and responses with care. Encourage your manager to speak objectively about your strengths, weaknesses, aspirations and potential. You need this specific information. Your communication strategy should focus on getting it.

"Listen more, talk less" may be another worthwhile communication strategy for this session with your manager. He got to the next level. His job outranks your job as assistant (whether or not it is a more satisfying job is debatable). Your manager might know things you don't from experience and from knowledge he has access to that you don't. He may have a bigger network than you (although administrative professionals should have some pretty big networks too). Work with your manager's ideas and thoughts. Listen up.

Take this information you get away in your head and figure how it works into your career path (if you have one yet) or next career management move. And it's worth repeating, keep building your business relationship with your manager or executive. Make it a win-win business relationship for both of you as much as you can. Your manager or executive is one of the best people to help you with your career aspirations and to be an ally to you in that way. Your manager is also someone who can get in the way of your next most desired career move. Maintain those "bridges."

***

Chapter 10 Recap:
- It's okay to ask for things you want in your administrative career because it is your career and you define it.
- You can ask others to help you get what you want.
- The worst response you can get when asking for something you want is "no," and that's not bad. That's life. Go about

getting what you want in a different way if that happens. Change your objectives, not your goal.

- If you want funding to attend a conference, ask for it – especially if there is a return on investment for the company investing in you to go to it.

- When you ask for what you want, express yourself assertively and not meekly.

- Make sure you phrase your questions to get the answers you desire. When you're not assertive, sometimes you ask things indirectly and incorrectly for your intentions. Managers answer your questions but it's the wrong responses because you asked the wrong questions.

- Always do your background research for any proposal prior to presenting it – whether asking for funding for a conference or a raise in your salary. You don't have to present everything you learned, but you need it on the backburner to answer potential questions about your proposal.

- Face-to-face communication is best for asking for what you want but sometimes e-mail will be appropriate for your situation and that's okay too.

- If you want a raise, ask for it. You may feel intimidated asking for more of someone else's money. A case of nerves is normal. It's still your right to ask.

- In most cases, you should only ask for a raise based on your own merits – not what someone down the hall makes who's doing the same work with the same skills.

- Things like 20% increase in workload and broadened responsibilities are reasons to be considered for a salary increase. Outstanding accomplishments are raise-worthy.

- Even when your proposals for your wants are met with negative responses, you should still say, "Thank you for your consideration." Request input for meeting your goal next time.

- Your best ally for your career aspirations is your boss. He's not necessarily a mentor, but you can gather advice from your manager or executive and support for your career pathway.
- If you have career path aspirations, discuss them with your manager or executive. He may not have a clue otherwise. He can't help you if has no clue what you're thinking.
- When you ask for feedback, don't get defensive. Listen more, talk less (except for asking for clarification). Say thank you.

Chapter 11

Communicating With Questions

Sometimes you may not get a useful response from someone you support or report to because you didn't ask the right "type" of question. The other person answered appropriately with the type of response that matched your type of question — one that didn't lead to the information you really wanted. So in order to get a useful response, or more efficient one, you must thoughtfully phrase your question; you can't count on mind-reading to clarify what you really meant to ask. In other words, to get useful responses, ask the right type of questions. Below are two common ways of phrasing questions.

Two Types of Questions

Closed-ended questions — This type of question often can be responded to with "yes" or "no":

Would you like to be the one to present the employee excellence award at the company luncheon Friday at noon?

Did you have a chance yet to look at the draft I gave you for the letter to the committee members?

Do you want me to take over collecting that information for you from your direct reports?

Is it okay if I schedule meetings on your calendar for Friday as long as they end by 4 p.m.?

Or perhaps you'll have the listener select one of two or three choices:

Do you want me to write a long, detailed report or simply a one-page report recapping the highlights of the event?

I'm making dinner reservations for you and our VIP guest. Do you prefer restaurant A or restaurant B or no preference between the two?

When flying, do you prefer the aisle seat or the window seat?

The Pros of Closed Questions: This type of question is good for getting specific responses and clarity on subjects. This is especially good when you're short on time or when you don't want to encourage discussion. This type of question is great for harnessing typically rambling type speakers.

Caution: Don't use closed-ended questions when you're really looking for more discussion. For example, "Is there any chance I'll get a raise this year?" is a closed-ended question. It leaves the door open for the responder to easily say, "Unfortunately, no." Then he or she changes the subject and smoothly moves onward, leaving you to ponder your real question, "What can I do to earn a raise this year?" Ask the right question to get your intended response.

In the earlier example about the letter to the committee members, you might really be meaning to ask, "What items can I help you complete now so you'll have time to review the draft letter to the committee members before 4 p.m.?"

These examples lead into open-ended questions.

Open-ended questions — This type of question can be thought-provoking or used for gathering information:

What do you think about the proposal I gave you for creating documented advancement paths for administrative professionals within our company? How would you improve upon the proposal or concept?

What can I do in my current role that will situate me for a larger salary increase or merit bonus?

How would you describe your work style?

How should I respond to Tom Stevens the next time he calls? He's already called five times in five days. Each time I ask him if I can help him or to leave a message, and he just keeps saying he'll call back tomorrow.

What are some good career books you've read that you think would benefit me to read too?

What commitments or promises did you make during the meeting that I can help you follow through on?

The Pros of Open-ended Questions: These open-ended questions are good for encouraging the other party to elaborate. They don't "allow" the other person to close the discussion with a simple one-word answer. Also, these questions show interest in the other person's opinions. Plus, the responses to these questions can give you background you may need on a topic.

How to Listen to Ask Effective Questions
Ironically, the art of asking effective questions involves being quiet. Even more than being quiet, it involves what's called *active listening skills*. Here are a few tips for listening after asking a question:

Pause after you ask the question.
Perhaps count to five slowly (and silently) if you have a habit of filling "dead air." Wait for the response.

Listen carefully to the response.

Don't "read" things into the response and wording. Ask a follow-up question if needed such as this: "So let me confirm that I understand correctly. In summary, I'm hearing you say, [fill in the blank]. Am I correct?"

Don't react defensively to a response to your question.

Such a reaction doesn't encourage future responses and may make any future questions you ask ineffective because people won't be forthright. They'll just say what you want to hear because you're now a known "issue" they want to be done with.

Your goal ultimately is to receive *authentic* responses to your questions because that's the type of information that's going to be useful to you. Therefore, you need to be open to real responses. There is no guarantee they will be correct responses or likeable responses. That risk exists when you ask questions or ask for feedback. So be it.

If someone is willing to give you feedback or authentic responses, grab all you can get – especially if it's from a credible or trusted source. If it's an "unknown" source, still embrace the response and mull over it. Use your judgment when on the receiving end of communication to keep or use what's reasonable and disregard (silently) the remainder.

Learn to Accept No Gracefully

As stated above, when asking questions you may not always like the response that you get. That comes with the territory of communication if it's to be true two-way communication. It was suggested in an earlier section that if you get a "no" such as related to a career goal, don't necessarily give up the ultimate goal and keep striving for a "yes." That's good advice with striving for career goals but not always good advice for communicating with managers, coworkers, colleagues or others with whom you come into contact.

For instance, you ask a close-ended question as described in this section as mandating a yes or no response. For this particular question, you're seeking a yes response. But the answer is no. Gasp! Learn to accept that no gracefully. It's that person's right to say no as much as it is for the person to say yes.

Positive assertion says not only can you say no, but so can the other party with whom you're communicating. Therefore, it's a bad communication strategy to be sullen when someone says no, and to speak back or write back (if e-mail) a response that portrays you as unable to accept no. That's not much different than a scenario in which you react defensively to feedback that's negative when you asked the other party for feedback.

As an example, I sometimes get e-mail requests to reprint articles I've written in newsletters exclusive to my administrative subscribers. A lot of times I say no to the requests (because the articles are *exclusively* promised to my readers or customers I explain). And in return, I get a whiny follow-up e-mail from the requestor with passive aggressive communication style (if not outright aggression).

For instance, the requestor portrays me as ungrateful and greedy for not allowing her to bestow the honor upon me of reprinting my existing work. Sometimes I also offer alternatives with my "no" such as to provide free brief interviews if the person wants to write her own original article, or I offer some short original material for her newsletter. Usually, the requestor doesn't even acknowledge I offered these alternatives. Instead, she gets stuck on my "no" and responds abruptly or passive aggressively and with a total lack of grace insinuating I've done something wrong by saying no.

Yet it's my right to say no, and it is your right too. However, if you can't accept no gracefully and with respect toward the other person, you hurt your own professional image. You also possibly affect future outcomes for other scenarios in those business relationships.

For instance, when I receive unpleasant "back talk" after I've said no, that makes me just want to close the conversation and make a mental note to not get into conversations or correspondence again with this person. Who has time for pettiness in business communication (or personal communication)? Plus, it's a distraction causing you to have to shift gears mentally to refocus on your work after an unpleasant communication.

Some people can't say no nor accept no. If you're in a business environment, you must learn to accept no gracefully and respond to it gracefully. If you can't do that, you *will* "burn bridges." That is not a good communication strategy. You will close the door with the person with whom you are communicating who might down the road have said yes to your next request.

I know of business deals occurring this way. Someone said no or simply didn't respond to a request because the person on the receiving end was busy or not interested at the time. The requestor didn't take "no" or "no response" personally. Later in the year or next year that requestor asked something else relevant to the same person in business and got a yes and good things happened. Sometimes the timing is just off. Sometimes it wasn't possible to meet your need. Next time it could be.

The same goes for administrative professionals asking for increases in salary. Sometimes no is the answer. Sometimes "no" simply means "not now" when you read between the lines.

Yet some administrative professionals will ask for a raise because someone else is making more in the same office; if and when the response is no, the administrative professional abruptly quits (or gives notice) – with no new job in hand. True story (or should I say "stories" as I've heard it more than once). Really! That's a sullen response to no (and one lacking in common sense and strategic thought).

Don't close workplace or business relationships with bad communication strategies like whining after you get a no or just no response. Control your emotions and use your brain for good. Not "reacting" to the word no spontaneously will give you an edge in your administrative field and career over others.

Good communication strategies keep doors open for you and help you to get the results you want next time if not this time. Communication is about exchanging information, not necessarily only communication you want to relay or hear. You don't get to script the entire communication – just your part, if that.

***

Chapter 11 Recap:

- Phrase your question with care so you get the type of response you're seeking. Otherwise, the other person may answer your question, but you won't get the information you sought because you didn't phrase your question properly.
- Close-ended questions call for responses of yes or no. Or you may ask the other person to select from multiple choice responses that you supply.
- Open-ended questions require elaboration such as opinions from the other person.
- If your manager rambles or you need specific clarity on a subject, use a close-ended question. If you want more input and discussion, use an open-ended question.
- An effective question requires active listening skills on your part (especially for open-ended questions). Deliberately pause to let the other person respond, listen carefully to the response without making assumptions, repeat what you heard for confirmation if necessary, and behave in a neutral manner and not a defensive manner to that response.
- You may not always like the response that you get to a question. That's okay. This is two-way communication, which is about exchanging information and not necessarily only communication you want to relay or hear.
- If you get a "no" to an open-ended question, accept it gracefully. While it's good to strive for a "yes" response to such things as career goals and to keep going after the yes from different angles, that's not always the case for yes/no questions. Sometimes no means no.

- Respect the other party's right to say no just as that person should respect your right to say no to a request. Don't react negatively to "no" and burn bridges within your own career and relationship network.

Chapter 12

Communicating By E-mail

Communication strategies apply to writing as well as speaking. In fact, you may find you spend more time communicating in writing, such as by e-mail, with some of your supervisors, coworkers or other business associates than by speaking with them face-to-face, by phone, or even by video conference. Yet it's no easier to communicate strategically in writing than orally, nor is it harder for some people.

However, even if you consider yourself to be quite articulate, persuasive, or even entertaining in oral conversation, you may communicate poorer by e-mail because you don't know how to convey your thoughts succinctly and clearly in writing. Also, you can't convey nonverbal gestures in writing which count for a lot in face-to-face communication. Using cute emoticons in e-mail in business correspondence can't replace face-to-face gestures. Besides, you shouldn't use emoticons in business correspondence of any kind if you want to appear professional. ☹ "Cute" isn't really a word that you should think of when you think of "business correspondence." ☺

In order to communicate strategically by e-mail, you must think before you choose e-mail as the appropriate communication format for your specific needs. Then you must think again before you write your message (and certainly think before you press the Send key). Below are some tips for communicating wisely and strategically by e-mail.

When or Why to Choose E-mail

What's more important than knowing *how* to write an e-mail is knowing *when* to write an e-mail. E-mail is a mode of communication, and different business situations call for different modes of communication. Choose your modes of communication wisely to help ensure effective communication as well as efficient usage of your time and the time of those you plan to communicate with.

For instance, if your message will require lots of two-way discussion, a telephone or in-person meeting would be more suitable than e-mail. If you're disseminating one-way information for which you're not expecting a lot of questions, then an e-mail would be a suitable communication mode.

Another good time to use e-mail is when you're distributing information that you want to remain accurate such as travel directions, step-by-step processes, and company policies. Relaying this information by phone or even in person may result in some steps being left out. By sending this information through e-mail (therefore in writing), you deflect the recipients asking you questions already answered and allow them ample opportunity to re-read the information until they comprehend it. If you've posted this information on your Web site, your e-mail may just point the recipient to the URL. The e-mail also provides a documentation trail and reminder that you sent the information to the recipient.

Likewise, if you have complex information to disseminate such as reports or proposals, you can communicate that information by e-mail; if it's long, make it an "attachment" in the e-mail, not part of the body of the e-mail message. Or reference an URL on your Web site to locate the document, or host it on a Cloud storage service and provide access to it.

This can be even better than sending paper reports because today many people prefer paperless (and this preference saves your company money on paper too). Many administrative professionals no longer distribute paper copies of long reports at meetings. Instead, they distribute the electronic copy or the URL location. Recipients can print their own copies if they prefer a paper copy and bring it to the meeting. Make the document a PDF file format so everyone can open it regardless of their software.

Another usage for which you might think e-mail is the best mode is for setting up meetings among multiple parties. You're right; it's good for that — but hold off on the *best* rating. Whatever mode of communication is most effective for completing this task is the best mode. Not everyone reads their e-mail promptly or responds just as quickly. When necessary, pick up the phone to facilitate meeting coordination. Likewise, when the phone option is not getting the job done, send that e-mail. Try one and then another, but don't bombard recipients with multiple forms of communication at once. It's not necessary to call someone to say: "Check your e-mail; I just sent you a timely e-mail about a meeting I'm coordinating."

If it's urgent, pick up the phone or stop by your coworker's office. If it's private, speak in person (e-mail is never guaranteed private between just two people). Give your communication mode deliberate thought. Sometimes the right communication tool is e-mail, and sometimes it's not. See Appendix H for a comparison table of the different digital communication modes with suggestions on when to use them, or not.

How to Form and Format Your Message

So you've decided e-mail is the right communication format to convey your message in the workplace. Now you need to write the message and write it well. After all, the best communication strategy is writing to be understood; that's a precedent to getting the results you are trying to achieve by your communication strategy.

And that brings us to the question of "What is it you're trying to communicate?" in this instance by e-mail. What is your core message? What result are you seeking? Some people also refer to *result* as your *objective*. Answer those two questions and you're on your way to crafting a useful piece of communication.

The responses to those two questions are the start of organizing your thoughts and planning your e-mail communication. The responses may even lead you to decide the best communication strategy is a communication mode other than e-mail. Assuming the best format is e-mail though, here are examples of responses to those two questions:

Your *core message* is you're compiling a report for your executive of department quarterly sales figures and need input from the department chairs. The *result* you want is the submission by all department chairs of their quarterly sales figures in a consistent format by Monday, June 23.

Your *core message* is you want to notify all staff that the building will be closing early on Friday, July 6, for site-wide pest control services. The *result* you want is for everyone to understand that they are expected to leave the building before then and not re-enter it until the time you state in your e-mail.

Your *core message* is that you are seeking feedback from staff on current meeting room options in order to evaluate if supply is meeting demand and determine if the facilities are adequate for the staff's needs during meetings. The *result* you want is for staff to specifically rate and comment on the location, layout, availability, furnishings, and audio-visual offerings for each meeting room you list and submit their comments to you by Friday, August 30.

Draft such notes for yourself each time you sit down to write an e-mail and you will soon find you are forming a clear and concise message because clarity and communication strategy starts in your brain. Therefore, write or type these notes to yourself (i.e. your brain output on paper):

My core message for this e-mail is this: _____.

The result (objective) I want for this e-mail is this: _____.

When considering your core message and desired results, also *think about whether you are writing to inform, persuade, explain, or gather input.* Knowing this will help you to clarify that result and write your e-mail in a style intended to meet it. So add this to your planning notes:

I am writing this e-mail to do this: [e.g. inform]_____.

As you then progress with writing your e-mail based on your fill-in-the-blank notes above, you'll need to add details to your message body. While doing this, picture yourself on the receiving end of the e-mail message and consider what questions your recipients might have about the core message and results (objective) you stated above. Then answer those questions within that e-mail as part of your message narrative. Or respond to potential objections, for instance, if you are writing a persuasive e-mail message. That's your message body. Your imaginary recipients are telling you what to put in your e-mail message in general; they need you to write the specifics which they don't yet know.

So now you have the content of your e-mail and know why you're writing it and what you intend to achieve by writing it.

Next, you need to consider your *audience's communication reception style*. And this is where "format" or layout of your e-mail comes into consideration. This is strategy to help you relay that core message and get those results you desire.

For instance, if you are writing an e-mail to your executive (or other executives) and it contains a lot of complex matters or details, then you might write an executive summary at the beginning of the e-mail. The assumption here is that busy executives in general want the bottom line as the first line (or paragraph) of their reading material. Then if a particular executive has more questions or desires more information, she will keep reading (or if this were an oral conversation, she would ask you specific questions).

You might use this same format for other audiences too because it's not just executives who want it quick; think of your busy, harried administrative colleagues too. Below is a potential example of an e-mail with an executive summary statement.

Example

Executive Summary:

A report and financial spreadsheet are attached regarding the annual golf tournament held this past Friday, May 2. The annual golf tournament event was deemed a success by its company organizers based on four pieces of data: 1) Golfer registration participation increased 20% over last year; 2) revenue increased 17% over last year; 3) issues that arose during the event were minimal, such as a single broken golf cart and two-minute delay of tee times; and 4) 85% of the evaluation forms collected from this year's participants reflected positive feedback.

The event leaders recommend having this event again next year in the same format, with the exception of changing the event time period to include the Memorial Day holiday weekend; this is to allow for more attendance from potential registrants who said they couldn't get off work to participate. The event leaders are seeking your input and/or approval on this suggested new time period. They also seek your approval for the same $30,000 budget with an addition of $50 per each additional registrant next year, not to exceed 50 more registrants than this year (due to space and tee times on the golf course).

Continue onward here with the body of your e-mail – not the executive summary, which you just completed, but the longer message that elaborates on the points made in the executive summary above.

Or that executive summary may be the entire e-mail if your elaboration is in the attachments. Put your points in the executive summary in the same order as they are made in the longer elaboration on the topic in your e-mail body (or the same order as they are in the attached report, proposal, business plan, etc.).

Also, depending on your intentions for the objective of your message and knowing your audience, you may have wanted to lead in the example executive summary above with the second paragraph (the request for approval for next year's dates and funding).

You decide the order of your content using your own judgment based on your audience and your intended message. In the example, you also considered the event leaders' intended message that you are relaying as the assistant to your executive. As an assistant, sometimes you have to make those judgment calls about what to put first in front of your executive's eyes, and what next. You have that power; use it wisely when communicating on behalf of your executive's direct reports or others to your executive.

Keep your executive summary to the point and short. Include in it a summary of what's in the longer body of your e-mail, such as the statement of need (or the problem), background information, analysis and main conclusions. Write all of that concisely in one or two paragraphs at the start of your e-mail.

You also could put this executive summary in an e-mail to which you attach a long document (e.g. proposal, report, business plan). Or include an URL that leads to such a document that you've placed in Cloud storage or on your company's Web site. It may be that you're attaching multiple documents such as various sales reports. The one executive summary refers to all of those documents; don't write an executive summary in your e-mail for each separate document.

With an executive summary, you assume that your busy executive may choose not to read further into the body of your e-mail or the attachments. However, you still need to write the e-mail body with care because he may read it. You also should assume that your executive may make a decision based on just your executive summary. So choose what you include in it with care. Communicate strategically. As an assistant, this executive summary is a great way to maximize your executive's time.

Another way to deal with complex or dense information in an e-mail body is to write a brief Table of Contents (TOC) and place it early in your e-mail, such as after the sentence that introduces the topic. Below is an example in which the TOC explains that an e-mail covers these items, in this order.

Example

The payroll department is instituting new procedures for time card submission [*your core message*], and all employees need to be in compliance with these new procedures beginning with the next submission date of June 2, 2014 [*your objective/results desired*]. The information you need to know is discussed in detail in this e-mail.

Summary of Topics Below:
1. New format for completing time cards
2. Authorized signature requirements
3. Schedule of dates for submission
4. Contact information for any questions

Details:
1. The new format for completing time cards is....[put your details here].

2. Authorization signatures are required on all time cards. You should sign your time card on the indicated line, and your direct supervisor should sign...[put your details here].

3. The date of submission for the time cards has changed from weekly to biweekly. The new calendar is... [put your details here].

4. If you have questions about the information contained in this e-mail, or if you have questions any time during the year related to your time card completion or pay check....[put your details here].

Notice that you followed the brief TOC with the details, using the same numbering format for each section of your e-mail that contains the related details. Now your readers know what the e-mail contains and can skip to sections they need to read or read again. Plus your e-mail is formatted clearly. Of course, you'll still need to write the details in each of those sections clearly too. So don't get sloppy with content once you've laid out an easily understood e-mail format; your word choices matter too.

The *executive summary* and *TOC* methods described above work for those e-mails, but it's not the only format for conveying a detailed message per e-mail. For instance, if you're writing to a customer with details about how to activate a product or submit a help request, then you'd want to write your e-mail in step-by-step, chronological order. The customer recipient of this e-mail needs more than the bottom line upfront in the e-mail unlike an internal executive or someone already familiar with some of the details.

And this customer recipient doesn't need a TOC of what he's about to read. This customer e-mail recipient needs hand-holding and help that starts from the beginning of the topic and completely walks him through the procedure. So what would be a tedious e-mail message style for one type of audience member may be the perfect writing style for another type of audience. Therefore, you must consider your audience for each e-mail message you write.

In this instance of the customer who needs detailed help with a process, you're going to write steps or sequences in your e-mail. A good way to do that is to use numbering or write "STEP 1," "STEP 2," and so forth. Separate each step or other item into its own paragraph with a blank line in between. This makes it easier to read and grasp the message.

If you are writing a message with *lengthy* bullet point statements, put a line break between each of those bullets too.

If you add an URL for whatever reason in your message, put the URL on its own line and with a blank line above and below it. This surrounding white space makes it easier to see. This format is perfect for complex steps or other information that needs to be followed and viewed clearly in an e-mail. See how this looks:

Example

There has been a malicious hacker attack on our server hosting abc customer relationship database software for clients. There is no evidence that the hacker actually accessed or downloaded any information from our clients' software accounts. That backdoor entry to the hacker has now been closed.

However, to be proactively cautious, all customers currently using the abc software need to upgrade their security measures immediately, including changing your password. Here are the steps to do everything you need to do to re-establish security measures within your account:

STEP 1 – Go to your administrative panel. You need to be on the Web to reach this console panel. The URL you need to reach the console online is this:

URL here (Consider making this a live URL so your recipients can just click the link.)

STEP 2 – Once you click that link (or cut and paste it into your Web browser and go to it), a dialog box will appear asking you to input your username and password. Do that now. Then click OK in the dialog box.

STEP 3 – Once you've provided the correct username and password and clicked OK, the administrative console for the abc software should appear on your screen. If it does not and you receive an error message, repeat steps one and two above and re-enter your data carefully ensuring no spaces and that your keyboard caps lock is set appropriately.

STEP 4 – keep adding steps as needed.

Communication strategy in e-mail means think before you write (type) about all of the elements of your intended message and your intended recipient in order to get the results you want. That's communication strategy! E-mail should not be a "brain dump" onto a page; those are the e-mails you're on the receiving end of that appear as though someone rolled out of bed and dumped their thoughts randomly onto a page and clicked Send.

Tips for Conveying the Message You Intend

Some e-mail messages can be cold, confusing, complex, and seemingly lack courtesy – even when that was not the writer's intention. Don't be that writer. Don't write those e-mail messages. Purposefully take steps to ensure that your e-mail messages don't have those negative attributes. Those unfriendly attributes hinder the intended reception of your message. That's not good communication strategy. Instead, consider all of the elements that go into conveying your e-mail core message and obtaining your intended results (objective).

For instance, acknowledge the person you're writing by name in your e-mail. This is called a salutation. It's a good way to give warmth to your communication.

Watch your "tone" in e-mail. It may seem to you that you're just writing directly your message or need in the e-mail. To the recipient, it may seem you are commanding him to do something or that you are unappreciative of something. The way around this is to insert words and phrases as appropriate like *please, thank you,* and *I appreciate that.* Try to write in a positive tone and conversational style while still keeping it business and not casual in tone.

Write in uppercase and lowercase letters, not solely one or the other. All caps should never be used to write an entire e-mail message or large portions of it. That is because all caps in e-mail is considered a way to shout in writing and express anger. All caps also shouldn't be used in most paper correspondence with the exception of putting emphasis on a word, or two or three consecutive words. The reason for not using all caps on paper isn't anger but rather that dense consecutive usage of all caps is hard to read in print.

In the e-mail example given earlier, you may have noted the use of all caps but sparingly such as to distinguish a complex list or sequence by writing STEP 1, STEP 2, and so forth in an e-mail body. Using all caps on just the one word like that in front of a bullet point or sequence step was simply to make the e-mail easier to read and the content clearer.

Another option could be writing the word in uppercase and lowercase but using bold, such as by writing **Step 1**, **Step 2**, etc., at the beginning of each item. Bold, like all caps, also shouldn't be overdone in digital or print communication, again because too much at once is hard to read. Likewise, if you're using bold for emphasis, then using too much would have the opposite effect. That means if everything is emphasized with bold (or caps), then none of it is seemingly more important than the rest.

Also, break your narrative down into short paragraphs. Long paragraphs, even ones seemingly fine in a print book, are hard to read on a computer screen (and even harder on a small tablet or smartphone screen).

If possible and when appropriate for your material, use easy to read layout. This was portrayed in some of the examples above that showed steps (or long bullet points) on separate lines with spacing above and after steps (or bullets), URLs, and short paragraphs. Very short bullet points don't need extra line spacing.

What might seem a bit of a choppy layout for print material, one even with excess white space, can be a superb layout for digital material. For instance, while the print copy of this book doesn't use block formatting or double spacing between most paragraphs for the text, that format *would* be appropriate for an e-mail. That is because it is very hard to read e-mail on a computer screen that is one long narrative with no white space. In fact, some people might not read a poorly formatted and dense e-mail at all (or they will try to skim it, thus missing parts). And that would defeat your communication strategy.

Finally, sign your e-mail. At the very least create a signature in your e-mail app so that it "magically" appears every time you write an e-mail. Then you don't have to worry whether or not you forgot to add your name with a closing. You can always change the signature manually in an e-mail in which you don't want it the way it appears in your automated signature.

Overall, your communication strategy for e-mail message creation should cover the words you use and the format and layout of those words on the page. This all makes your message more readable and understandable, even courteous. In turn, that helps you get the results you're seeking from your communication. That's what communication strategy is all about. Put thought into the entire e-mail communication production. If you don't, your ultimate e-mail may be wasting your time and that of the recipient. That's not good, especially in business. Communicate strategically with your e-mail.

***

Chapter 12 Recap:

- It's just as easy – or hard – to communicate in writing, such as by e-mail, as it is face to face.

- You can be a great communicator in person and not so great in writing, or vice-versa.

- In person, you can use nonverbal gestures to communicate. You cannot do so in writing. Do not try to substitute emoticons for those nonverbal gestures; emoticons have no place in professional business correspondence.

- What's more important than knowing *how* to write an e-mail is knowing *when* to write an e-mail. Before forming your message, you need to decide which mode of communication is right for conveying your message. E-mail is a mode of communication just as is a face-to-face meeting or an instant message.

- If you choose e-mail as your communication mode, write your message well. To do this, know your core message and desired result (objective).

- Also think about whether you are writing to inform, persuade, explain, or gather input so you can best write your e-mail to meet the desired result.

- The center body of your e-mail contains more details about your message. One way to fill this information in is to think about what questions your recipients might have about your core message and objective and answer those potential questions here.

- Also consider your audience's communication reception style. This will help you decide whether to put the bottom line first or proceed with an orderly, step-by-step detailed e-mail.

- E-mail is not a "brain dump" onto a page. Think before you craft your message, as you're crafting your message, and again before you click Send.

- Use a salutation to add warmth to your e-mail communication. Also, take care to use words that convey a courteous, positive tone in your message.

- Use short paragraphs in e-mail and put deliberate thought into any formatting such as when using bold or all caps.

- Put adequate space between paragraphs and long bullet points in e-mail messages.
- Good use of layout and formatting is necessary to make your digital material more reader friendly. That in turn works toward getting your message heard and understood. Being heard and understood is always necessary and most certainly so if your objective includes getting a response.
- Sign your e-mail. Create an automated signature in your e-mail app if you don't want to create a signature for each e-mail.

Chapter 13

Other Electronic Forms
of Communication

E-mail communication is still widely popular in the business world but no longer the only form of digital communication for business professionals. There is also instant messaging, online chat, text messaging and online discussion forums. At one time some of these were considered "fun" communication tools that employees should not be using on company time. Fortunately, times are changing as more employers get educated about the benefits of these communication tools for business usage and by their employees.

These electronic communication tools all serve good purposes for the right types of communication in the workplace and in your career. Learn them, use them, but use them wisely. As repeated throughout this book, communication strategy starts with thinking; use planning to form your message and choose the best communication mode for it (digital or not).

Instant Messaging and Online Chat

To some people instant messaging is a quick way to relay a simple request and get a speedy answer. It's a convenient way to communicate. To others, in particular some people on the receiving end, an instant message equates to an interruption. Which is it for you and which is it for your recipient? Think before you instant message – or interrupt – a coworker, colleague or manager. Each communication situation with instant messaging calls for independent judgment in regard to its appropriateness. Only you know your message and its recipient's work style.

For instance, look at my scenario. I'm writing this book. It takes focus and a one-line train of thought to write these chapters. Suddenly an instant message appears on my computer screen (if my IM were turned on) asking me if I can speak at an event in Smith Town on February 2 on the topic of e-mail management. Will I welcome that communication and be in the frame of mind to say yes to it?

Not likely. I'll see it as an interruption. I have to stop what I'm doing to respond. Then I'll take several minutes to refocus my train of thought on what I was writing. Perhaps I'll even have to re-read the last few paragraphs before I can continue onward with this writing project. I would have much more appreciated the communicator contact me by voice mail or e-mail. The latter would have allowed more room for details too instead of a Q&A chat session back and forth. However, the communicator thought she was just sending me a quick message to check my availability, and so why bother sending an e-mail for that. But her agenda was not mine.

This same scenario could apply to that coworker in your office a few doors, or cubicles, away from you working on a report. You think it's silly to form an e-mail for your question which just needs a simple yes or no. Likewise, you think it's a waste of time to get up from your seat and walk down the hall for that communication (and besides, you're waiting on a visitor and need to be at your desk). So you decide to just send an instant message. That way you'll get an answer now, unlike if you had to wait for your coworker to read your e-mail and respond on her own time. So you instant message your coworker, and you get a response – yes – so everything must be good. You can check that inquiry off your to-do list too.

Oh, but you just thought of one more quick follow-up question, so you'll send another instant message. It's short. It'll only take your coworker three seconds to respond, you think. And that may be true. But it may take her another 15 minutes to refocus her thoughts on the report she is writing or to re-add that column of figures she was in the middle of calculating when the instant message popped up on her computer screen. Sure she could have ignored it, but once it's there, it's there. Your brain sees it. Sure she could have turned off her instant messaging alerts, but she forgot (or the company management requires it stays on).

Therefore, you put thought into your communication strategy but you forgot to think about your audience's preferred communication mode. That's part of communication strategy too because you want your audience to be receptive to your message and its objective. Use instant messaging and online chat but use it wisely and strategically. It's a good thing, but too much of a good thing isn't always good either for various reasons.

Think of instant messaging as a communication mode that's good to use when you need an immediate response and one that isn't going to take a lot of back and forth communication. It also could be used in the office to send a routine reminder that you know the recipients would appreciate: "Reminder: R&D Meeting in the conference room starting in five minutes."

Don't use instant messaging when face-to-face communication or e-mail would be a better option for the message and the recipient – even if not for you as the sender. This is business. Sometimes you have to cater to the communication preferences of those with whom you do business. That is the best communication strategy for your current objective and long-term business relationships in the office, or elsewhere. Think strategically. Communicate strategically.

Text Messaging

If you communicate with your manager or executive (or other staff you support) by "telephone," you may actually mean by text messaging, not speaking on the phone. This is becoming more popular as a communication mode between assistants and those they support. For instance, you text your manager or executive while he's traveling with directions or contact information needed to help him get to his next appointment (hopefully, he knows better than to actually check the text message on his cell phone while he's driving though). Or your executive is on a trip, and you text him about a few phone calls he needs to return. Or maybe your executive is simply down the hall in a closed-door meeting, and you text him that he's behind schedule and his visitor and next appointment is waiting in the lobby.

Even if you as the assistant don't have a company cell phone, you can still send a text message to your executive's phone by e-mail or over the Web from your computer. The good thing about text messaging your executive (or others in the workplace) is that many people (way too many) are tethered to their phones by an invisible cord. Therefore, if you have a timely message to send to your manager or executive, then it's likely he'll take notice fairly quickly. Of course, if you've established a communication routine together for when to send and expect text messages, he'll notice them even quicker (e.g. send me a text if I'm running late in my meeting, and my next visitor arrives on schedule). That's communicating strategically in the sense of strategically choosing your mode for the specific communication.

Text messaging rightfully has a growing spot in the workplace environment for communicating messages appropriate for that mode of communication. For instance, some companies send text messages to their off-duty employees about shift and schedule changes or start times. I know this firsthand as sometimes my spouse gets these messages. It's non-intrusive compared to a ringing phone, especially when he's taking a nap. If you're trying to get a short message to your executive when he's asleep in another time zone and you're awake and in the office, text messaging could be your best choice.

Plus, as an assistant when you send your message about whatever it is you think is important and timely enough to text, you have documentation that you sent it. Sometimes you may need that documentation as proof you did what you said you did. Or maybe the text document serves as a reminder to yourself on a busy day that you took care of the matter at all or correctly.

As far as phrasing your text messages, words still matter. In this case, length does too. It almost goes without saying that you should keep your text messages short. Reading text on a phone of any size can sometimes be a challenge for some people. But it's not the best place for reading a full-length proposal. If you want to send the URL to that proposal to your traveling executive so he can access it on a larger device later, you can do that; just don't try to send the entire multi-page proposal as a text message. If your executive chooses to check his own e-mail over his smartphone, so be it; his choice and issue if the content is dense wording.

Also when writing a text message, put the most important information in the beginning of the text, keep to the point, and don't write something that needs a lengthy or complicated return message.

Since your message is a professional business matter, also use good grammar and writing skills. Don't use a bunch of sloppy grammar and text abbreviations or acronyms (which your manager or executive may not even understand). In other words, don't write "Ur DW called, Plz pick up DD, 3 p.m." and "DW called back, said nvm, thx."

If your company uses text messaging, make sure you know any policies surrounding its usage. Or establish a policy or rules with your manager for not using it as well. For instance, there may be safety issues involved with texting certain types of employees (e.g. floor production workers, drivers, heavy machinery/equipment operators). If your manager asks you to get in touch with such employees (who are "on the clock"), then consider your options and timing if you're thinking of using a text message.

For example, send your text during known shift breaks, send it to the person's supervisor or dispatcher to notify the employee, or go see the person face-to-face if he is in another area of the company such as on the production floor.

On the other hand, a good company policy on texting should have already notified such employees when to and when not to check text messages, in which case you can send your text any time; just don't expect the person to read it immediately. In this case, if immediate results are your intention, you're using the wrong communication strategy. Choosing the right communication strategy for relaying a message entails consideration of the message content and type, the communication mode, and the audience's availability and access to that communication form.

Online Discussion Forums

An online discussion forum is an online place ("bulletin board," if you're familiar with that term), where you can leave a message and get responses from group members. You participate in a discussion there, not necessarily in real time. Or you can just go there to read messages (i.e. comments, posts or threads).

Online discussion groups are also one form of online social networks. To benefit from these to the maximum, you need to engage versus lurk (i.e. just "listen" and read). When you're engaging in online social networks, you are communicating. So utilize communication strategies for online discussions the same as with any other form of communication. That is if you want to convey your message and meet your communication objective.

For instance, you want to post a message in an online discussion group for administrative professionals (of which there is one for *The Effective Admin* brand at LinkedIn). As with the e-mail communication strategies mentioned in the last chapter, you should plan before you post (i.e. *share* your *discussion* or *comment* within the group). If you are starting a new discussion, ask yourself the same questions you do when planning to write an e-mail: What is your core message? What is your objective (results you want from the message)?

Your responses to those two questions will dictate what will go into the body of your comment for a new discussion thread. Don't ramble. Be to the point. Keep it concise. The discussion/comment box will have a maximum word count; stay within those bounds, which may allow you several hundred words. If you go over word count, a message will usually appear that states you can't post successfully until you shorten your comment.

Use as many words as you need to convey your core message and objective clearly and adequately for group members to understand. Otherwise, you may not get many (or any) responses, and if you do get responses, it may be group members asking you to elaborate or clarify your discussion comment or question. If you communicate strategically (think before you post), you will have answered most prospective questions within your original discussion comment.

When writing your discussion post, use proper spelling and good grammar and sentence structure. Thousands of people, such as professional colleagues, coworkers, and prospective employers may see your message, even perhaps your current managers and executives depending on the particular composition of group members. Writing in a professional manner for an online business discussion forum reflects on your perception.

Plus proper spelling, good grammar, and good sentence structure is a communication strategy to ensure people understand your message. This strategy helps ensure you get results from your message.

An often overlooked area in regard to starting a new discussion in an online forum is the topic headline (subject line). Carefully choose the words or phrase that you put in the topic headline. This is vital to strategically communicating in online discussion forums. This is the first thing you will write in your discussion post and the first thing group members will read.

In fact, it may be the deciding factor in whether or not busy professionals even stop to read your post and reply. People these days are scanners. Many will skim the headlines (subject or headline topic in this case). If they understand your topic headline and think they can help you or if it interests them, they'll open the thread and read your post in full. If not, they'll put it off until they have more time, or they won't open it and read it at all.

So just like with e-mail, your topic or request needs to be in the subject line (topic headline). Perhaps this is especially more so with group discussion than e-mail because group members may not personally know you. At least with an internal work e-mail or one to an off-site colleague, the recipient probably knows your name. Therefore, he or she will give you a "pass" if you write an irrelevant subject line and still open your e-mail. In a group discussion forum, most of the members probably don't know you (unless it's an in-house company group forum). Most won't give you "a pass;" they'll just pass up reading your discussion. That probably wasn't your communication strategy intention.

So write a straightforward, specific, concise and meaningful topic headline in group discussions. This will maximize your chances of getting responses to a new discussion you start.

Don't try to write a clever and catchy headline. Most group members probably don't want to or won't think about what your cleverness means. This is because busy professionals don't have time to wait for you to get to the point. For every clever headline that does attract attention to a discussion, many more likely do not do so. Therefore, don't do "clever" in your discussion headline unless you're willing to accept the risk of minimal responses to your post or delayed responses.

Group Forum Topic Headline Examples

Not So Good: Calendaring.
Better: Tips needed for organizing a new executive's calendar.

Not So Good: Resume assistance needed.
Better: Can you review my resume, please?

Not So Good: Who's watching you online?
Better: Synopsis of an article about maintaining your privacy online. Let's discuss.

Not So Good: Minute taking help needed.
Better: Is it okay to use audio recorders in minute taking?

Not So Good: Women Executives...ugh!!!
Better: Is it harder to support a female executive (vs. male)?

Not So Good: Job interview help needed.

Better: How do you answer "Tell me about yourself" in job interviews?

Be specific. Be upfront with your needs (objective). Some people who post in discussion forums write a mysterious topic headline. They follow this with a rambling post that ends with a final sentence which contains their true core message and objective. Their "last sentence" should have been in the topic headline and/or mentioned at the beginning of the comment.

To communicate strategically, you need to communicate in an organized and clear manner. Think before you post to online discussion groups. Your comments are valid, but they need to be understandable and respect readers' time (which will benefit you too).

After you post a new discussion thread in an online group forum, stick around. You don't have to be online constantly, but come back daily to check the discussion thread. Interact with other members in the discussion. At a minimum, thank people for coming to your aid and responding to your discussion. It's a polite gesture for letting group members know you're appreciative of their taking the time out of their days to answer your question or join in your discussion. This is also a good communication strategy if you want to maintain the online professional relationships you are building and be perceived as a professional.

You may start discussions in professional online forums on any topic you wish as long as your topic is relative to the group's core purpose. Peruse and study existing comments in the forum, and read the group rules to understand the group culture and purpose. Then jump in.

You may also respond with comments in existing discussion threads. This is good if you have something relevant to add that's not already been stated. However, sometimes it is okay to repeat your agreement with a previous group member's viewpoint; it depends on the topic and question. You judge the situation. Regardless of what you post, continue to communicate with professionalism. Define what professionalism means to you in order to do that.

By participating in professional online discussion forums, you may help others, get help with your own issues or questions, build new business relationships, and even get noticed by potential employers (after all, you're staying visible in a business or career-related environment). This is like networking in a face-to-face professional network meeting, except it's virtual and not real time.

Despite those differences, you'd be wise to treat the two professional network formats similarly. That is if you're participating in an online "professional" discussion forum (such as LinkedIn, but there are others too). If you're participating in an online hobby discussion forum, you may choose to be casual and not business professional. You'd still be wise to remember that what you post reflects on you (and may be seen by people within your professional circles too).

Also, no matter whether you're writing in a professional or nonprofessional online discussion forum environment, you are still writing to be read and understood. You're still trying to communicate. So much of the rules that apply to communicating in a professional online forum can apply to a more casual one too. Consider making good communication strategy part of your entire life – at work and when you're off work too.

***

Chapter 13 Recap:
- E-mail is no longer the only form of digital communication that is popular or widely accepted in today's business environment; so is instant messaging, online chat, text messaging and online discussion forums. Determine the right mode of communication for your message and your audience.

- An instant message might be a speedy way for you to get an answer. In some cases though, it's also an interruption to the recipient. Therefore, use instant messaging wisely, not constantly.

- Use instant messaging only for short messages needing short responses.
- Text messaging can be a good and useful business communication mode, including between manager or executive and assistant. You can send travel directions, phone messages, and reminders about upcoming appointments.
- Since most people are tethered to their mobile phones, you can send a timely message by text and expect it to be read pretty quickly.
- Keep text messages short and put the most important information in them upfront.
- If you're sending a text message in a business environment, avoid using lots of slang and text abbreviations or acronyms. Your message is a professional business matter.
- If your company uses text messaging, make sure you know your company's policy for its usage. Or establish a policy or rules with your manager for not using it as well. An example is when using it could create a safety issue for certain types of employees reporting to your manager.
- Online discussion groups are one form of online social networks. To benefit from these to the maximum, you need to engage versus lurk (i.e. just "listen" and read).
- Utilize communication strategies for online discussions the same as with any other form of communication. If you want to convey your message and meet your communication objective, then plan your message before you post or click Share.
- Write a straightforward, specific, concise and meaningful topic headline in group discussions to maximize your chances of getting responses to a new discussion you start.
- Also put your question or needs (objective) upfront in the body of the post. Don't make group members read a rambling post only to get to your core message and objective at the very end.

- After you post a new discussion thread in an online group forum, stick around and interact in it. Thank group members for taking their time to reply to you.
- By participating in professional online discussion forums, you may help others, get help with your own issues or questions, build new business relationships, and even get noticed by potential employers.

Chapter 14

Communicating With Professionalism

Your conduct, attributes and intentions all contribute to your professionalism and whether you will act like a business professional and be perceived as one by those with whom you work. A professional is an expert in her field and behaves like one. An administrative professional is an expert in the administrative field. The administrative professional role requires interpersonal skills. This skill involves communicating with professionalism, which will be apparent in your written and verbal communications.

For instance, the quality and appearance of your written communication reflects on your professionalism. The courtesy you use when communicating reflects on your professionalism. Also, the tact and diplomacy you use when communicating reflects on your professionalism. Below is more information on these three topics.

Grammar, Punctuation and Spelling Matter

Readers can tell a lot about you – or at least they think they can – from your writing. "At least they think they can" means perception is reality. People will form an image of you based on what they read from you. That image may not be true, but it's based on all they have to go on. The mind instinctively forms images of other people from whatever it has to go on. In this case, that's your writing.

So if your writing is eloquent, readers may think you're a good writer (and they will understand the message you're trying to convey); they may also think you're intelligent, organized and knowledgeable. Contrarily, if your writing is sloppy, they may think you lack attention to detail or don't pay much attention at all to what you're doing or with whom you're corresponding. If your writing is full of errors, readers may think you lack knowledge or literacy. Those are not good traits for the image of a business professional and especially not for an administrative professional.

Therefore, how you write is not only a communication strategy important to conveying your core message and obtaining its intended results, but it's also a strategy for defining your professionalism and image in the workplace (and in your career overall). You must remember the saying that "business is not casual," and apply it when communicating in the workplace environment in writing in any communication mode (i.e. print correspondence and digital communication such as e-mail, IM, chat, texting, and online social networks that are professional in nature). Refresh grammar, punctuation and spelling skills ongoing throughout your career.

Since this is a book about communication strategies for administrative professionals and not specifically about grammar, punctuation and spelling, you will not learn those specifics here today. Instead search Amazon.com or other bookstores for this topic. There you will find excellent books such as my old favorites like *Woe Is I* by Patricia T. O'Conner and *When Words Collide* by Lauren Kessler and Duncan McDonald. New books on these topics are added every year. Consider the customer reviews to help you judge if you're getting reputable information before you make your purchase. Consult my favorite dictionary too: *The Merriam-Webster Dictionary*. If you don't want to buy your own copy, use its Web site: http://www.merriam-webster.com/

Courtesy Counts in Communication

If you want people to be receptive to your communication, you need to be clear and courteous. If you want to build relationships in your workplace and career network, you need to communicate courteously. If you want to communicate with professionalism, you need to communicate with courtesy. Simple guidelines can help you to be more courteous in your communications:

- Say or write please and thank you.

- Don't communicate jokes in which you're not the butt of the joke.
- Don't communicate anything in the workplace that can be construed as offensive.
- Remember that your priorities, timelines and deadlines aren't always that of the recipient of your information or requests.
- Don't interrupt, whether during face-to-face communication or by sending an untimely instant message.
- Pause to listen.
- Ask for clarification rather than making assumptions.
- Use the right mode of communication for the message. Don't call a face-to-face meeting for something that can be broadcast by e-mail. Pick up the phone instead of initiating a long conversation by instant message or text.
- Consider using your audience's preferred communication mode.
- Be respectful of other people's time; don't ramble when speaking or writing.
- Respect other people's opinions and values, while realizing you don't have to share them.
- Give your undivided attention when communicating with others; don't multitask by working on unrelated activities.
- Maintain confidential communications out of respect for those who confide in you.
- Take the time to learn how to spell people's names correctly; don't guess.
- End face-to-face conversations, phone conversations, and e-mail with a courteous closing; don't just abruptly stop in e-mail, or hang up the phone or say, "Uh, huh, bye."
- Only write comments in the virtual world that you are sure you would say to the same person if you met him or her on the street.

- Acknowledge people who take the time to help you, give you advice, or give you feedback.
- Don't yell, whether out loud or in all caps in digital communications.

What else can you add to that list?

Tact and Diplomacy and the Assistant

Assistants often don't have positional powers or authoritative powers to communicate information, requests and needs to get results. Instead, assistants use tact and diplomacy to do the same thing.

Actually, even if you have positional or authoritative power, you should still communicate with tact and diplomacy. That's part of communicating with professionalism. That's also part of your communication strategy to get the results you need from your communications with others.

So how do you do this? You do it with thought and sensitivity. Here are some suggestions and scenarios you may encounter in your administrative or assistant role that would benefit by tact and diplomacy:

Leverage your executive's authority strategically and sparingly.

This applies to when delegating work on behalf of your executive to others, or requesting information from them. In other words, don't constantly imply, "I work for the [executive title], and therefore you need to respond to me – now."

Instead, just be considerate and candid about your needs – and always specific. That'll work much of the time. You want to create goodwill and harmony and have people react and respond positively to your needs, and to the image you carry with you as a proxy for your executive. This will do more good for you long-term as a communication strategy than utilizing what is essentially scare tactics or demands.

Fortunately, most high-level executive assistants already know this conduct. If you're up and coming to the role, you may be surprised to learn, happy to know, and glad to emulate this communication strategy based in using tact and diplomacy and not from any authoritative power. When your executive's direct reports see you coming or your name show up on their phones' caller i.d., they should break out a genuine smile, ideally. That's how you'll make progress in forwarding your executive's agenda and gain cooperation in doing so.

Be empathetic.

When a coworker or manager is telling you about an issue, listen to understand, not necessarily to agree with someone. What's important to that person may not be important to you. Regardless, if you can genuinely empathize, you may be able to help that person talk through her issue and resolve it. You're using empathy but also tact and diplomacy. Not doing so would be saying, "You need to toughen up and work it out. That's necessary for the nature of this job. Now get going. I'm busy."

Contrarily, empathy is the ability to understand and relate to that person's feelings. It's you saying: "That must be scary for you to know you're going to speak in front of 2,000 people the first time you give a presentation. That's what I call 'jumping right in.' Been there, done it, didn't like it. I believe you'll get through it well enough though."

It's empathy, not sympathy; therefore, it's you saying "I can relate," and not "I am so sorry this is happening to you and that you have to do this speech."

On the other hand, perhaps you are somebody who does not typically feel empathy – I do believe some people are more empathetic than others – and therefore, you cannot relate; in that case, strive for understanding: "I understand what you're saying – that it's difficult for you to do xyz. Can I help you prepare somehow?" In times that call for empathy, lift coworkers up, not down. Encourage, don't discourage. Help coworkers find solutions and strength within themselves.

Also use sympathy when appropriate.

For instance, you may have a situation in which a coworker or manager is grieving a death or coping with a sick relative. Or maybe the person lost an account or lost out on a promotion. Now is the time to be tactful with what you say: "I'm sorry this is happening. If you need to take some time off at any time, let's discuss a few tasks before then that I can handle for you while you're away that would be helpful. I might not be able to do many, but I can do some."

Also, be discreet. Don't announce someone's bad fortune to anyone else – including your manager or executive – without a really good reason.

Recognize and acknowledge other people's viewpoints diplomatically.

That means you say: "So you believe that it would be more effective if we divided up the responsibilities for the project instead of collaborating simultaneously. That may be an idea worth exploring further. Can I share my prospective game plan with you too?"

Don't start off with negative statements such as "Oh, we did that and it didn't work," or "That doesn't sound like a good idea to me." If someone shares a viewpoint, that person must think it's useful or valid. Don't outright say it's not: "For your own good and to keep you from embarrassing yourself, I have to be direct with you and flat out tell you that your idea stinks. Bottom line."

That's not being tactful or diplomatic. There is direct and there is too direct. That's too direct. While that example phrasing might work for dramatic effect on a television reality show, it doesn't work well in true reality in the workplace. Use tact and diplomacy to encourage ongoing communication sharing, but also to reject or massage ideas you think aren't so good. Some other tactful or diplomatic phrasing might be "From another perspective..." and "May I point out that..."

Acknowledge and respect leadership, authority and expertise.

Some people in high positions in your company have them because they know something that perhaps you don't. Those with expertise in certain skills or with dealing with certain situations also may know something you don't. (Likewise, you know a lot that they don't in the administrative expertise realm.) Use tact and diplomacy if and when you decide to question those other people's decisions or input. Many will welcome your "push back" when done tactfully and diplomatically and with respect for the position or expertise.

For instance, your executive gives you an assignment. Because you are a proactive thinker, perhaps intuitive too, you realize she's possibly "missing something" with her thinking. Rather than say, "I think you better re-think that [even though you've been successfully handling matters like this for your 20-year career]", you might say this:

"I'm going to start on that task right now. Do you think we also should notify the marketing department? I remember you explaining to me once the effectiveness of internal collaboration when someone is working on a complementary project, and I know the marketing department is doing something on this topic too."

When you use tact and diplomacy in your communication strategy, you don't embarrass coworkers, managers or executives when correcting them or pointing out something that's perhaps obvious but they've failed to see it. To do this, you also give this push back, as well as any potentially negative feedback, in private for an audience of just two.

The same goes for if you're giving feedback to your executive's direct reports. Handle it with tact and diplomacy and as a matter for two sets of ears only. Always be aware of who else is potentially in hearing range when you deliver information of any kind to anyone in your office. What you say, how you say it, and where you say it are all important to your communication strategies.

Final words: Communicating with professionalism reflects on your personal brand – your professional image. Additionally, since you are an employee of your company, your professionalism reflects on your company's professionalism and those you support (e.g. executive). As an assistant, you are often viewed as an extension of those you support (and you actually are that too).

Therefore communicating with professionalism is critical to performing your administrative role and representing those you support in the workplace. Communicating with professionalism should be part of your overall communication strategy in your role and career.

***

Chapter 14 Recap:

- Your conduct, attributes and intentions all contribute to your professionalism and whether you will act like a business professional and be perceived as one by those with whom you work.
- The administrative professional role requires interpersonal skills, which involves communicating with professionalism – whether in writing or orally.
- Readers of your written correspondence will form a perception of you based on your writing. It doesn't have to be reality but it will be their reality of you.
- How you write is a communication strategy important to conveying your core message and obtaining its intended results, and also a strategy for defining your professionalism and image in the workplace.
- Your writing could be in an e-mail or in an instant message, text message or online forum. Remember that business is not casual no matter the communication mode if it's pertaining to a business environment.
- Refresh grammar, punctuation and spelling skills ongoing throughout your career.

- To enhance the reception and understanding of your communication, be clear and courteous (regardless of the communication mode). The list for doing this is long, such as saying or writing *please* and *thank you* or restraining an urge to interrupt in a face-to-face communication.
- Use tact and diplomacy in your business communications. It adds to your professionalism and aids you in getting a response.
- Using tact and diplomacy may mean deliberately not verbally leveraging your positional power (if you are an EA to a CEO, for example), being empathetic or sympathetic when appropriate (two different things), recognizing and acknowledging other people's viewpoints diplomatically, and acknowledging and respecting leadership, authority and expertise.
- Communicating with professionalism reflects on your personal brand – your professional image – and also the brand of your company and your manager or executive that you directly support and represent to others.

Chapter 15

Communicating Forever

Communicating never ends. Only the chapters in this book on communication strategies stop here. The chapters do not cover every communication scenario for the administrative professional role and career. That would be impossible – unless this were renamed "The Very Big Book of Communication Strategies for Administrative Professionals" and it contained hundreds of pages. What's covered are some of the more common scenarios in the work days and lives of administrative professionals requiring communication strategies. Try the communication strategies from the previous chapters. Fine-tune them and make them your own.

Also understand that though you are at the end of this book, you are not complete in your studies of communication skills for the work environment. You are not a master of strategic communication yet. You may never be at the master level. You will constantly be challenged in the workplace and in your career with new and ongoing situations requiring you to communicate strategically. That means *think before you speak* in order to get the results you're seeking through your communication. What comes out of your lips makes its way there from your brain. Use your brain to communicate strategically.

***

> You're at the end of the chapters but not the end of this book. Continue onward to the appendices for lots more useful information related to the chapter topics in this book.

Appendices

Appendix A

Additional Words and Phrases to Use or Not

Through the years, I've published various words and phrases in *The Effective Admin newsletter* intended to help administrative professionals know what to say in an awkward situation, get clarity, or be perceived better (because your words and phrases impact others' perceptions of you). Since these words and phrases are not limited to one subtopic in the body of this book but rather are a mishmash of useful words and phrases to say – or not to say – I've randomly reprinted a compilation of some of them below for you to use in your workplace.

Three Words or Phrases That Can Improve Your Image and Workplace Relationships

1) Please; 2) Thank you; and 3) You're welcome.

So simple, right? Pass it on!

Three Phrases That Will Make You More Popular in the Workplace

1) Tell me more; 2) What do you think? 3) What are your thoughts on this issue?

Good open-ended questions or phrases (like the ones above), sincere interest in the responses, and active listening skills can make you smarter and create a positive perception of you by those with whom you interact. People will seek you out more because you listen to them and seek their point of view and expertise. Therefore, you will become more popular as an indirect effect of doing this. Try those phrases in your next one-on-one person conversation.

What to say When Someone Restates Your Idea in a Meeting as Theirs

"That's building on my original suggestion, and I like your tweak on it; I concur."

An Unprovocative Response for Offensive Humor

Say: "I didn't get it. Could you please explain what makes that funny?"

Two Phrases to Help You Avoid Personal Gossip

Someone comes to you with personal information about your coworker. You'd like to politely decline interest in hearing it. Try saying one of these phrases as soon as possible to halt the conversation:

- I don't believe that information concerns me, so I'd rather not hear it (or, so I'd rather not hear any more about it).
- I'm not comfortable talking about that. Let's change the subject.

Giving Specific Praise to Your Manager or Executive

Nonspecific: Boss, you did a great job giving that presentation. I really enjoyed listening to it.

Specific: Boss, you did a great job giving that presentation. I particularly liked that point you made about ABC. I never thought of doing something that way. But you've inspired me to do XYZ.

How to Respond to a Compliment

With two words: "Thank you."

Don't display low self-esteem or lack of confidence by adding statements like, "It was nothing," or "It really wasn't that big of a deal."

The Right Way to Say "I'm Sorry"

Say "I'm sorry" like you mean it. E.g. "I'm sorry I said xyz to you"; not "I'm sorry you misunderstood me."

Also, don't use e-mail as a crutch for making apologies. It's easy to blurt out something inappropriate or wrong; it's a lot harder to come back and apologize in person. If you "write" an apology, do so because that's best for the situation — not because you don't want to face the person.

What the #%&@ do You Mean? The Potential Consequences of Swearing at Work

Employers are inclined to think less of an employee who swears at work for a variety of reasons. Most (81 percent) believe that the use of curse words brings the employee's professionalism into question. Others are concerned with the lack of control (71 percent) and lack of maturity (68 percent) demonstrated by swearing at work, while 54 percent said swearing at work makes an employee appear less intelligent.

Yet while many employers may think less of an employee who curses too much in the office, one in four employers (25 percent) admitted to swearing at their employees. Roughly the same amount (28 percent) of workers said they have sworn at other coworkers.

Source: CareerBuilder's survey of 2,298 U.S. hiring managers and human resource professionals and 3,892 U.S. workers. The survey was conducted online by Harris Interactive in 2012. This information was obtained from the July 25 press release at http://www.careerbuilder.com.

Learn How to Disagree Politely

What a person is doing or saying may not be within your morals or comfort zone but that doesn't make it right or wrong.

However, if you're in a conversation and don't agree with what the other person is saying, then here is what you can say:

"That's an interesting viewpoint I hadn't considered before. Thanks for sharing it with me."

That's just one way to respond without getting angry or escalating anger from the other person. You also don't compromise your principles, or say something hastily you'll later regret.

Substitute This One Word for Better Communication: *And* for *But*

By replacing the word "but" with "and" in some scenarios, you can keep your listener at ease and actually listening. That's because sometimes when you use *but* (for instance, when delivering feedback), your listener stops listening and starts mentally preparing at *but* for bad news or a complaint.

For example, which of these two sentences might be perceived better by the listener?

I enjoyed the group activities during the session *but* the size of the groups was too large to give each person a chance to participate;

or

I enjoyed the group activities during the session *and* think they will provide even more value to the participants if we make the groups smaller next time.

Word choices can change the tone of your communication.

Six Phrases That Won't Help You Add Value at Work

Don't get caught by surprise and blurt out one of these trite phrases, or excuses:

1. "They didn't get back to me."
2. "I didn't think that was my job."
3. "I thought someone else was taking care of that."
4. "No one ever told me."
5. "I didn't think it was that important."
6. "I didn't think to ask about that."

Instead, replace the above phrases with these thoughts and actions:

1. Do more, take charge, call again.
2. Over-deliver, exceed your job description.
3. Double-check, don't assume.
4. Inquire, get curious.
5. Don't judge without knowledge.
6. Anticipate.

Conversational Phrases That Hurt Your Credibility

Certain phrases you use to help you sound more conversational and candid can actually make you sound less credible.

For instance, have any of these variations slipped from your tongue: "to be honest," "to be perfectly honest with you," or "I have to be honest with you." What do you think when you hear those words from someone? That's what others think when they hear them coming from you.

Eliminate these siblings of those phrases too:

- To tell you the truth
- I'll be frank with you

Drop the "honest" preamble and just say what you mean. That's being candid.

Communicating With Confidence and Credibility

Increase your credibility by speaking more confidently and assertively.

Don't Say:

- I guess
- I think
- I hope
- It seems

- In my humble opinion

Do Say:
- I know
- I believe
- I will
- I get
- It is

How to be a More Confident Communicator
Don't weaken your communication skills by asking for affirmation of everything you say:
- Does what I'm saying make sense?
- Wouldn't you agree?
- Am I right?

How to Communicate With a Positive Tone
Create a positive tone in your oral and written communications by not starting your sentence with the word "no," and by utilizing "positive phrasing." Here's an example:

I wish I could help you with that. However, I won't be here that day.

That's better than saying: "*No. I can't* help you. Sorry."

Increase Your Influence With the Right Words
You can influence someone's cooperation or willingness to assist you, or desire to do something, with your phrasing. For instance, which would you respond to more positively: "Would you like to go to the dentist?" Or, "Would you like relief today for that pain in your mouth?"

Here's a workplace example. "Would you consider working overtime all this week to help me organize an event for 2,000 attendees?" Or this one: "Would you like to work on a project I'm leading that'll look good in your list of accomplishments for your performance review? Plus, it'll give you a chance to network with some people in our company that you might not know yet."

"Show" Someone You're Listening

Some people say "umm hmm," "I hear you," etc., in an attempt to demonstrate they're attentively listening and interested in what someone is saying. A better way is to ask a question related to what the speaker is saying: "What made you decide to xyz instead of abc?"

Another way is to restate the speaker's key points in your own words: "So you think I should put more of x and less of y in the report to make it more readable."

Appendix B

Differences and Similarities
of Behavior Styles

KEY: y = yes n = no When interacting with another person, ...	Assertive Behavior	Passive Behavior	Aggressive Behavior	Passive Aggres-sive Behavior
...you clearly and honestly state your opinion.	y	n	y	n
...you clearly and honestly state how you feel.	y	n	y	n
...you clearly and honestly state what you want.	y	n	y	n
...you violate the rights of that person.	n	n	y	maybe
...you get what you want at the expense of the other person.	n	n	y	maybe
...you manipulate the other person.	n	n	y	n
...you recognize and respect the opinions, feelings and needs of the other person.	y	maybe	n	n
...you're direct in your communications and behavior.	y	n	y	n

...you treat the other person's wants, needs and rights the same as you do your own.	y	n	n	n
...you plan to pleasantly agree with the other person publicly now and quietly get even with him or her later.	n	n	n	y
...your needs are met satisfactorily and so are the other person's.	y	n	n	n

Appendix C

List: Items for Career Portfolio

These are items you can include in your professional portfolio (*master* binder); this list is in no particular order:

- Resume
- List of references
- Recommendation letters from employers
- Recommendations reprinted from your profile page on LinkedIn
- Past and current job descriptions (you write them).
- Awards you've received or for which you've been nominated (relevant to administrative professionals; if not, then relevant to your administrative skill set or to attributes such as leadership, team player, etc.)
- Teams or groups you've been part of that demonstrate your involvement in teamwork; if they're not directly relevant to administrative work, emphasize that you've learned how to be a better team player and that it's something that transitions to your job as an administrative professional within a company.
- List of leadership positions (current or past)
- Samples of your past work and/or examples of work you're capable of doing with explanations in footnotes or annotations in margins as needed; also, if it's a "real" document, black out or change confidential information and names to fictional information and make sure that's apparent to readers.
  - Correspondence, such as thank you letter, interoffice memo/e-mail, agendas, minutes, invitation, process or procedure description/steps,

travel itineraries, report excerpts, etc. This shows your business writing skills and document creation skills plus formatting, grammar, punctuation, proofreading and other specific skills depending on the document and its purpose.

- o Software: Create and show PowerPoint presentation pages, Excel charts, organizational charts, project management charts, etc.
- o Desktop publishing: newsletter pages you've created, Web site pages, brochures, pamphlets, flyers, invitations
- o Social media: screen shots from social media pages you were responsible for creating and/or updating
- o Forms: travel expense statements, travel authorization requests, time sheets, and any other types of forms you've created
- o Spreadsheets, documents that show budget familiarity or creation
- Transcripts from schools and colleges
- Test results such as software tests from staffing agencies
- Diplomas from colleges
- Certificates of completion of training from any courses (paid or free ones)
- Certificates of competency (shows at what level you mastered the curriculum)
- Class outlines (demonstrates topics you had chances to become familiar with)
- List of organizations with which you volunteered or do so now (emphasize or highlight skills relevant to administrative professional positions)
- Membership certificates or list of organizations of which you're a member (relevant to administrative professional role or skills)

- Class outlines in which you were the instructor or co-instructor (or note your instruction portion if other instructors)
- Special projects you were part of and your role and perhaps what the group achieved
- Accomplishments; this could even be a bullet list of "top 10." For instance, money-saving initiatives, process improvement initiatives, time-saving successes, etc. If you have many, you could use category headings like those and list the top 10 per category per page.
- Task lists; tasks are not accomplishments but a one-page list of tasks you've done and can do might be useful; use bullet points and alphabetize the list for easy viewing.
- Letters of praise (letters, e-mails, note cards) for jobs well done, appreciation of your assistance, thank you notes, etc.

Appendix D

Table: Brainstorming Your Strengths

Chapter 4 discussed highlighting your strengths to use as support in your communication strategies to your manager or executive about what you can do. It may be that you want to do that in order to get more responsibility, interesting work, or the chance to work on a particular assignment.

Take some time to think about what are your strengths (knowledge, skills, attributes, talent, or innate ability), and how you can transfer them in the workplace to different types of tasks and assignments. For example, make a brainstorming chart like this but with your own content:

Knowledge, Skill, Attribute, Talent, or Innate Ability You Consider a Strength:	*Potentially Enables You to Do This:*
Good with math	✓ Manage and maintain department budgets ✓ Shop for bargains on equipment and supplies ✓ Help with the creation of financial spreadsheets
Party planning pro	✓ Coordinate special events ✓ Formulate activities to build team spirit and morale

Patience	✓ Handle "high maintenance" customer situations ✓ Teach novices computer techniques (or other skills) ✓ Train volunteers
Breaking things down for people in simple terms	✓ Create standard operating procedures manuals (or other technical manuals for customer or employee usage) ✓ Teach segments of in-house training classes ✓ Orient new employees to our workplace culture and routines
Reading comprehension	✓ Read and highlight the "important stuff" for your manager from his reading pile backlog ✓ Read complex how-to directions and relay them to managers and coworkers quickly to enable them to do something ✓ Write the executive summary for or a synopsis of a long report ✓ Curate relevant research information from online publications for your manager's usage
Using online social networks	✓ Respond to customer issues on Twitter ✓ Update the company's Blog ✓ Collect useful data/research from social network posts ✓ Create an internal Blog

If you have an administrative "buddy" at work or if you hold meetings of administrative professionals, then help each other by brainstorming and assessing each other's strengths and thinking of ways these strengths can be transferred into new workplace opportunities (as noted in the table above). Sometimes it takes another person's perspective to point out what you're good at. You may have strengths that you take for granted or think aren't useable in the workplace. A helpful coworker or colleague can tell you otherwise.

Appendix E

Goal Setting Formula

If you are setting a workplace goal – whether it is a stretch goal or not – consider using the SMART goal setting formula.

SMART is an acronym that stands for Specific, Measurable, Achievable, Realistic, and Time-related.

A goal is a statement describing a result you plan to achieve (through an action).

You simply make the goal SMART.

Here is a SMART goal example:

Creation of a budget for the 2016 Customer Appreciation Conference by March 30, 2015, that does not exceed $15,000 in expenses while maintaining the quality standards assigned to last year's conference.

- ✓ **S:** You have included *specific* details in the goal and a *specific* result desired.
- ✓ **M:** You have included *measurements* (also specific) that identify when the goal is achieved.
- ✓ **A:** You have made the goal *achievable*, basing it on reasonable or attainable resources and scheduling, and financial and quality constraints.
- ✓ **R:** You have set a *realistic* goal because you have the knowledge and skills to achieve it, such as financial acumen to deal with budgets and familiarity with past conference expectations and standards.
- ✓ **T:** You have set a *time-related* deadline for achieving the goal.

Appendix F

Manager Onboarding Sheet
From Assistant

Perhaps proactively create a one- or two-page quick "cheat sheet" to give to your new manager or executive. Use tact and diplomacy skills when doing this. In the cheat sheet, explain your goal and expectations for the working relationship and what you can or will do in terms of assistance. Here's one way to write it:

My goal: To assist you in ways that maximize your time and free you of any administrative tasks and assignments that fall within my administrative management expertise and realm.

My expectations: We will continuously communicate to develop mutual trust and respect in each other and fine-tune our working relationship to a business partnership, figuratively speaking. You will let me know ongoing what I'm doing well and is working for you, and also what's not working for you and needs improvement. That's so I can do more of what's working and try to fix what's not.

Potential assistance I can provide to you (in no particular order and * by my above average strengths):

- PowerPoint presentation creation*
- Manage and organize your e-mail, even respond to some per your style
- Complete scheduling and calendar management
- Drafting correspondence in your preferred style
- Online research and content curating
- Proofreading
- Maintaining budgets*
- Merging and maintaining your personal calendar with your professional calendar

- Serve as a gatekeeper to filter your incoming visitors, callers, and information to your benefit
- Act as a proxy for you in meetings you can't attend
- Be a second set of eyes and ears and note-taker in meetings to which I accompany you
- Tech guru and troubleshooter as needed to help you manage your technology gadgets
- Meeting and event planner
- Travel arrangements coordinator
- Write more bullets here as needed.

Appendix G

Salary Resource Web Sites

http://www.officeteam.com/salary-center
http://www.GlassDoor.com
http://www.PayScale.com
http://www.Salary.com

Appendix H

Table: Comparing Communication Modes

Chapters 12 discussed when or why to choose e-mail as your communication mode. This choice is part of your communication strategy. Many communication modes exist to choose from today including the four in this table: e-mail, phone, face-to-face and instant messaging. Not covered is text, video conferencing, Web conferencing, and more.

While this table is not all inclusive, perhaps it'll give you some thoughts to add to when deciding on the best communication mode for your message. In particular instances in your workplace or career, you may choose to disagree with the suggestions below. That's okay. Use your judgment because exceptions always exist to what might usually be the norm.

Possible Usage	E-mail	Phone	Face-to-face	Instant Message
To convey complex messages (steps, procedures, directions)	Yes	Maybe	Maybe	No
To convey confidential information	No (or at your own risk)	Yes	Yes	No
To convey sensitive information	No (or at your own risk)	Yes	Yes	No
For close-ended questions (i.e. yes/no, multiple choice)	Yes	Yes	Yes	Yes

For open-ended questions (requiring opinions, elaboration)	Maybe (depends on extent of elaboration needed)	Yes	Yes	No
For one-way broadcasts to multiple people (i.e. announcements, open invitations not requiring rsvp, general information)	Yes	No (exception: pre-recorded information the audience calls in for on demand)	No (because no response or Q&A to follow; if Q&A, then yes but for a group meeting only)	No
For two-way conversations entailing much dialogue	No	Yes	Yes	No
To relay information to someone in a different time zone	Yes	Maybe (depends on times in both places)	Maybe (depends on times in both places and location)	Maybe (depends on times in both places and message length)

Perhaps you can tell by some of the notes in the table cells above that the lines are no longer clear for when to use e-mail, phone, face-to-face or other communication modes.

For instance a decade or so ago, almost nobody did on-demand audio or Webinars (pre-recorded). Instead there were live conference calls only at set times. You were either on the telephone call live or you missed your chance to hear the conference call (however, if you were lucky, a transcript of the call was available to read or someone took minutes). Now, information that used to be broadcast live can be disseminated as replays or pre-recorded audio or video over the Web and listened to or viewed on the individual audience member's time (e.g. a training seminar).

Another example is in the past you might travel to meet someone face to face whereas now that same meeting can be held live online including with a live Q&A chat session in real time. You don't even need to leave your office desk and computer to meet *virtually* face to face with someone. However, you can still miss out on some nonverbal gestures by not being truly face to face with someone. Yet this is still a good option for many conversations and meetings in which you actually want to see the person with whom you are speaking.

So think about technology's role in your communication strategies. Changes in technology can lead to changes in your communication strategies. It's no longer a question of simply should I visit, call, or write a letter. Technology has given us more options to communicate to anyone at any time and any place. What hasn't changed is that you still have to use your judgment to decide which communication mode is best for your particular message, objective and audience. No technology can advise you or make that decision for you.

Appendix I

Additional Resources for Admins

Virtual Association for Administrative Professionals (VAAP)

How much better could you be in your administrative professional role if you had instant and ongoing access every day to practical advice, news, ideas and tips specifically relevant to your administrative job and career that you could put to use starting today?

Could you...

√... maintain or improve your job performance?

√ ...further impress your employer (or prospective employers) with your expertise?

√ ...better manage your career as an administrative professional?

√ ...implement new strategies and processes to increase the efficiency and effectiveness of both you and those you support?

√ ...come up with new ideas and inspiration you can tweak and call your own relevant to your work, making you a more innovative and valuable administrative professional in your company?

YES, you can do all that with the tips and knowledge available in Virtual Association for Administrative Professionals (VAAP) educational resources.

Resources include current subscription to *The Effective Admin newsletter* (digital) and access to all archives of the newsletter dating back to 2004; *The Effective Admin Tips Series* publications 1-22, special reports, membership certificate and more.

Get more details, rate, and join at http://www.thevaap.com

About the Author

Karen Porter is a virtual job performance and career success coach and advisor to administrative professionals globally and founder and president of *The Effective Admin* (TEA) brand of resources – serving thousands of administrative professionals since 2004. She founded a second brand, *Virtual Association for Administrative Professionals* (VAAP), in 2009 as a comprehensive online resource of job performance and career strategies and information for administrative professionals.

Porter also holds a Bachelor of Science degree in journalism and communications from the University of Florida. Through TEA and VAAP professional development and training resources and tools, she shows you how to be the best administrative professional you can be while getting the benefits and satisfaction you deserve as an administrative career professional. Based in Southeast Georgia, USA, Porter communicates virtually with assistants. Contact information is at her Website:

http://www.theeffectiveadmin.com/contact-info/

Made in the USA
San Bernardino, CA
21 February 2016